Animating Black and
Brown Liberation

Animating Black and Brown Liberation

A Theory of American Literatures

MICHAEL DATCHER

Cover art: Francisco Letelier.

Published by State University of New York Press, Albany

© 2019 State University of New York

All rights reserved

No part of this book may be used or reproduced in any manner whatsoever without written permission. No part of this book may be stored in a retrieval system or transmitted in any form or by any means including electronic, electrostatic, magnetic tape, mechanical, photocopying, recording, or otherwise without the prior permission in writing of the publisher.

For information, contact State University of New York Press, Albany, NY
www.sunypress.edu

Library of Congress Cataloging-in-Publication Data

Names: Datcher, Michael, 1967– author.
Title: Animating black and brown liberation : a theory of American literatures / Michael Datcher.
Description: Albany : State University of New York Press, [2019] | Includes bibliographical references and index.
Identifiers: LCCN 2018020076 | ISBN 9781438473390 (hardcover) | ISBN 9781438473406 (pbk) | ISBN 9781438473413 (ebook)
Subjects: LCSH: American literature—Social aspects. | Liberty in literature. |

Power (Social sciences) in literature. | Liberalism in literature. |
American literature—African American authors—History and criticism. |
American literature—Hispanic American authors—History and criticism. |
Agent (Philosophy) | Hegemony—United States.
Classification: LCC PS169.L5 D38 2019 | DDC 810.9/3552—dc23
LC record available at https://lccn.loc.gov/2018020076

10 9 8 7 6 5 4 3 2 1

Contents

Acknowledgments — vii

Introduction: Animacy Matters — 1

1 A Matter of Body and Soul in *The People of Paper* and *Mumbo Jumbo* — 39

2 Heroes and Hieroglyphics of the Flesh in *The Salt Eaters* and *Heroes and Saints* — 63

3 Animating Anthologies and Firing the Canon in *This Bridge Called My Back* and *June Jordan's Poetry for the People* — 93

4 Wanda Coleman and Kamau Daáood Sing the Blues for the Black Body — 115

Coda: The World Stage Performance Gallery Moves — 135

Notes — 139

Bibliography — 161

Index — 169

Acknowledgments

First and foremost, I would like to thank Drs. Erica R. Edwards, Vorris L. Nunley, and Tiffany A. López for their intellectual guidance and professional support, which were invaluable in the creation of this book. You have my most sincere gratitude and respect. I would like to thank Dr. Barbara Christian for believing in me enough to spend time with me as an undergraduate and for lighting the flame that now burns in this book. I am so grateful for June Jordan for demonstrating how an engaged artist and public intellectual goes about the people's work with a spirit of love. I am also grateful of Dr. Marci R. McMahon and two anonymous reviewers whose cogent insight considerably improved this manuscript. Dr. Monica A. Coleman provided an inspiring example of the scholarly life for which I was a beneficiary. I am thankful for Loyola Marymount University and the University of California Riverside for their institutional support. A special nod goes to the World Stage Performance Gallery co-founders Billy Higgins and Kamau Daáood for demonstrating and promoting excellence in the arts for the Black community and the world, to Executive Director Dwight Trible for continuing and elevating their vision through exemplary leadership, and to the members of the World Stage Anansi Writer's Workshop whose consistent output of excellent literary cultural production is a constant source of inspiration. I am grateful for the love and support that I have received from my mother Gladys Steen, my father Norman Avery, my sister Cynthia Datcher, and my brother Elgin Datcher. My young feminist daughters Eyerusalem Coleman-Kitch and Harlem Coleman-Datcher inspire me with their extraordinary courage, boundless creativity, and fierce commitment to the empowerment of girls and women: I am honored to be your father.

Lastly, I am deeply grateful for the wise Latina playwright, actor and educator Carmen Bordas O'Connor, my soulmate who loves me like she knows love is a verb.

Introduction

Animacy Matters

La facultad is the capacity to see in surface phenomena the meaning of deeper realities, to see the deep structure below the surface. It is an instant "sensing," a quick perception arrived at by the part of the psyche that does not speak, that communicates in images and symbols which are the faces of feelings, that is, behind which feelings reside/hide. The one possessing this sensitivity is excruciatingly alive to the world.[1]

—Gloria Anzaldúa

Why the pathology of race was so dominant a part of Western consciousness or what might be done to change that character was of less concern than how Black peoples might survive the encounter.[2]

—Cedric Robinson

At the risk of seeming ridiculous, let me say that the true revolutionary is guided by a great feeling of love. It is impossible to think of a genuine revolutionary lacking this quality . . . We must strive every day so that this love of living humanity will be transformed into actual deeds, into acts that serve as examples, as a moving force.[3]

—Ernesto "Che" Guevara

Liberation Vibrations

Why are embodied Black and Brown subjects (operating as racialized matter for this discussion), too often the targets of irrational violence? In particular, why are alarming numbers of unarmed Black subjects met with lethal force while interacting with the State-sponsored security apparatus? Why is lethal violence against Black and Brown racialized matter insufficiently punished? Why don't Black and Brown lives matter?

On August 3, 2013, the aforementioned questions animated a lively forum at Vibrations, a Black-owned, grassroots cultural center in Inglewood, California.[4] Housed in a storefront on busy Manchester Boulevard, Vibrations serves a working-class neighborhood with a primarily African-American and Latinx population. The cultural center regularly hosts poetry readings, sociopolitical study groups, book signings, musical performances, lectures, and community discussions. The August 3, 2013, forum was an intergenerational discussion and information-sharing session in response to challenges facing local and national African-American and Latinx communities, including, but not limited to (1) the February 26, 2012, Sanford, Florida, killing of unarmed Black 17-year-old Trayvon Martin by 28-year-old mixed-race Latino George Zimmerman, and the subsequent not guilty verdicts received by Zimmerman; (2) the "school-to-prison pipeline"[5] in African American and Latinx neighborhoods; (3) intergenerational miscommunication in African-American and Latinx communities, and the delimiting effects on social justice organizing work resulting from this miscommunication.

Another type of lively forum occurred on November 24, 2014, in Ferguson, Missouri. The outdoor rally addressed questions similar to the Vibrations forum. The intergenerational discussion and rally was a response to the forthcoming indictment decision regarding Ferguson, Missouri, police officer Darren Wilson who shot unarmed Black teenager Michael Brown. Michael Brown's mother, Lesley McSpadden, was a rally speaker. When a media-feed announced the non-indictment decision, a distraught McSpadden said to the crowd, "Everybody wants me to be calm. Do they know how those bullets hit my son? What they did to his body as they entered his body? Nobody had to live through what I had to live through . . . They still don't care. They're never gonna care."[6]

It is significant that McSpadden's comments focused on the impact of State violence on her son's Black body. The Black mother's interrogatives ("Do they know how those bullets hit my son? What they did to his body as they entered his body?") are an acknowledgment that the attack was an assault on an embodied Black subject, on Black matter. McSpadden recognized that the assault on her son's Black life was a "careless" assault, evidenced by her statements, "They still don't care. They're never gonna care." This perceived careless sentiment is echoed by other rally participants who can be heard shouting, "They don't care about us." "They don't care about us," can be read as the State does not value Black life: Black embodied matter does not matter.

Taken collectively, McSpadden's response, and those of rally members, echo concerns by some in the African-American community that the perceived, relatively low value of Black life is contributing to the startling phenomena of unarmed Black men being killed by the State's security apparatus. In 2014, State security forces killed the following unarmed Black men: Ezell Ford, Akai Gurley, Eric Garner, Mike Brown, Dontre Hamilton, Rumain Brisbon, and Charly "Africa" Leundeu Keunang.[7] The State's security apparatus's aggressive assault on unarmed Black male bodies has overshadowed its problematic relationship with Black female bodies. In July 2015 alone, five Black women (Raynette Turner, Joyce Curnell, Ralkina Jones, Kindra Chapman, and Sandra Bland) died in jail while under the supervision of United States jailers.[8] It was only after the online #SayHerName hashtag campaign emerged that Sandra Bland's case began to garner nationwide media attention.[9]

In the sovereign power[10] context, this study will analyze best practices, strategies, and challenges related to Black and Latinx subjects' sociopolitical and economic liberation, including gender's liberatory impact. The project will explore how the State's hegemonic efforts to push Black subjects toward bare life provides the framework for the State's efforts to push Latinx subjects and other marginalized populations toward bare life. Donald J. Trump's presidential campaign and post-victory rhetoric featured language that aggressively demonized African-American, Latinx, and other marginalized communities.[11] As the State's most powerful representative, Trump's rhetoric signaled an antagonistic attitude toward the aforementioned communities and suggested an openness to State policies that could push these subjects in the direction of bare life.

In conversation with Aristotle, Foucault, and Hannah Arendt, Giorgio Agamben's bare life notion interrogates the space between biological existence (*zoē*)—or "mere life"—and life tethered to political agency and speech (*bios*)—or "good life." Agamben argues, "The fundamental categorical pair of Western politics is not that of friend/enemy but that of bare life/political existence, *zoē/bios*, exclusion/inclusion."[12] In a more nuanced reading, Ewa Plonowska Ziarek asserts that "bare life, wounded, expendable, and endangered, is not the same as biological *zoē*, but rather the remains of the destroyed political *bios*."[13]

Alexander Weheliye proffers a generative critique of influential bare life discourses, especially as they relate to theorizing about racialized subjects. Weheliye writes:

> Bare life and biopolitics discourse not only misconstrues how profoundly race and racism shape the modern idea of the human, it also overlooks or perfunctorily writes off theorizations of race, subjection, and humanity found in black and ethnic studies, allowing bare life and biopolitics discourse to imagine an indivisible biological substance anterior to racialization.[14]

As an alternative to bare life discourses, Weheliye argues that a racial assemblage "construes race not as a biological or cultural classification but as a set of sociopolitical processes that discipline humanity into full humans, not-quite-humans, and non-humans."[15] Weheliye's racial assemblages idea leans on the work of influential scholar Hortense Spillers's "flesh" notion, of which this project will also attend. While acknowledging Weheliye's cogent bare life critique, this study will employ bare life discourse in conjunction with discourses that explicitly theorize about racialized subjects—especially Black subjects whose *bios* is targeted.

Their political *bios* targeted and destroyed, Black subjects like Michael Brown and Eric Garner can have their bare life, Black bodies destroyed without accountability because they have been "[s]tripped from political significance and exposed to murderous violence, bare life is both the counterpart of the sovereign on the state of exception and the target of sovereign violence."[16] The State qua sovereign's lack of accountability for killing Black citizens coheres with Agamben's understanding of *homo sacer*.

Agamben makes a genealogical connection between bare life and the archaic Roman law concept *homo sacer*, sacred man. "The protagonist of this book is bare life, that is, the life of *homo sacer* (sacred man) who may be killed and yet not sacrificed."[17] "May be killed" is a referent to sacred man's exclusion from the juridical order's normal operations regarding a citizen and the "unpunishability of his killing."[18] Sacred and expendable, Black life aligns with Anzaldúa's understanding of Coatlicue, the indigenous Aztec goddess. Coatlicue represents duality in life and "depicts the contradictory . . . she is the symbol of the fusion of opposites."[19] Black embodied matter is a fusion of opposites—desired and despised; the State seeks to mark Black bodies as spaces for violence and domination even while framing Black bodies as objects of difference and desire in the American imaginary. Katherine McKittrick avers:

> What is it about space, place, and blackness—the uneven sites of physical and experiential 'difference'—that derange the landscape and its inhabitants? . . . [R]acism and sexism produce attendant geographies that are bound up in human disempowerment and dispossession. This can be seen, most disturbingly, in locations of racial and sexual violence—dragged bodies, historical and contemporary lynchings, rape—wherein not only is the body marked as different, but this difference, precisely because it is entwined with domination, inscribes the multiple scales outside the body itself.[20]

When State-sponsored violence against Black bodies goes unpunished, it deranges the American landscape, because homicide operates, not as a crime, but as a building block to institutional State power. State security apparatus representatives, these sovereign representatives who killed Michael Brown and Eric Garner in 2014, in 2016, Philando Castile,[21] and in 2018, Stephon Clark,[22] are operating in "the sovereign sphere . . . in which [they are] permitted to kill without committing homicide."[23] Officer Jeronimo Yanez's July 2017 acquittal in the Philando Castile killing is suggestive of this permission to kill without committing homicide. As in the Castile case, Black matter, the embodied Black subject, the sacred man, is *operated on* in this sovereign sphere where Black life has been reduced to bare life—or death. This study is necessary, because there is a need to explore, as

Ziarek writes, "whether bare life itself can be mobilized by emancipatory movements."[24]

Animating Black and Brown Liberation reframes Ziarek's inquiry in the following ways. Among marginalized American communities (which the State often pushes toward bare life), what strategies can be effectively employed to animate emancipatory thought and mobilize emancipatory thought into emancipatory action? Can American literatures[25] function as a source of effective liberatory strategies for marginalized folk *operated on* in the sovereign sphere? What theoretical interventions, and practical applications, need to be animated in order that emancipatory strategies, found in literary-based cultural production, can positively influence marginalized communities material conditions, and mobilize their liberatory action? How can art-based counterpublics, and the people who inhabit them, animate liberatory thought and action? This study's liberation-related nomenclature is purposeful. The historic and contemporary sociopolitical and juridical forces operating on marginalized communities in the United States have had the practical impact of delimiting the life courses of significant numbers in these respective communities.[26]

Specifically, the process of mobilizing bare life Black and Brown subjects is confronted by a fundamental problem: When a subject is excluded from the good life, and is pushed to the societal order's margins, the subject can focus on mere life survival rather than emancipatory action. The survival orientation involved in "trying to find a way out of no way" can tack a subject away from the port of collective action, the port of all hands on deck. *Animating Black and Brown Liberation* argues that American literatures are lighthouses that can show a way out of no way. American narratives can illuminate new liberatory possibilities.

Erica R. Edwards writes, "Literature is a repository for counter stories and alternative visions . . . narrative is a dialogic site for reimagining possibilities." The counter stories of Cherríe Moraga, Toni Cade Bambara, Salvador Plascencia, Ishmael Reed, Gloria Anzaldúa, June Jordan, Wanda Coleman, Kamau Daáood, and others, are so rich in alternative imagination, and emancipatory vision, that they can help guide bare life subjects toward justice—even in the sovereign sphere.

Toni Cade Bambara's *The Salt Eaters* is a narrative that follows several community activists with ties to the Feminist, Civil Rights, Black Power, Chicana/o Power, and Anti-War Movements. The narrative is propelled by community activist Velma Henry's story. Henry has recently attempted suicide by cutting her wrist and placing her head in a gas oven. Burned-out from living bare life, death becomes an option. At the start of the novel, Henry is under the care of community healer Minnie Ransom who accesses indigenous African religious healing modalities in her attempt to heal Velma. Velma resists the healing to such an extent that Minnie asks her, "Are you sure sweetheart that you want to be well?"[27] Minnie Ransom's question can be understood as, "Do you want to be more alive?"

Theorists Jane Bennett and Mel Y. Chen's work engage the intersection of cultural production, race, and "levels of aliveness"—while employing nomenclature that seeks to problematize life and its sociopolitical concerns.[28] Chen writes, "Using animacy as a central construct, rather than 'life' or 'liveliness'—though these remain a critical part of the conversation in this book—helps us theorize current anxieties around the production of humanness in contemporary times."[29] Understanding the production and contours of Black and Brown humanness, the contours of Black and Brown aliveness, is central to this project. In contradistinction to ontological definitions of Blackness and Black aliveness rooted in enumerating brutalities, McKittrick argues that, "the brutalities of racial encounter demand a form of human being and being human that newly iterates blackness as uncomfortably enumerating the unanticipated contours of black life."[30] Coterminous with McKittrick's argument, this American literatures study interrogates how emancipatory action, freedom fighting, functions as an ontological prism in which to articulate unanticipated contours of Black and Brown life. In the sovereign sphere context, the State's (and its representatives) inability to accept Black and Brown subjects' full humanity, its rich contours, lays the groundwork for other American subjects to devalue Black and Brown humanity—and, at times, for Black and Brown folk to devalue their own humanity, their own level of animacy.

There is no standard animacy definition, but it has been variously described as "a quality of agency, awareness, mobility, and liveness."[31] Both Chen and Bennett couch their examination of animacy in a discussion of materiality. Chen imagines animacy "as a specific kind of affective and material construct that is not only non-neutral in relation to animals, humans, and living and dead things, but is shaped by race and sexuality, mapping various biopolitical realizations of animacy in the contemporary culture of the United States."[32] Bennett's goal "is to theorize materiality that is as much force as entity, as much energy as matter."[33]

Both Chen and Bennett explore the mapping of matter on animacy hierarchies. In this material hierarchy, as an example, a stone would be placed near the bottom of the animacy hierarchy, because it has relatively low levels of agency, awareness, mobility, and aliveness. Algae, dog, and human being matter would appear as we move up the animacy scale. At the human being level, Chen introduces race into the equation, offering human differentiation, and relative human value to the discussion, which is generative for this study. How and why is one human life deemed more valuable than another? Who determines the process of relative human value, how do value assessors assume this position of power, and what determinative technologies do they employ in the assigning of human value? Responding to Fanon's important sociogenic notion ("the always socialized nature of our modes of being human, and thereby of our experiencing what it is like to be human"[34]), polymath Black feminist scholar Sylvia Wynter, whose impressive scholarship and creative work have interrogated the intersection of ontology, race and culture for over 40 years, uses a sociohistorical and cultural frame to briefly outline the development of relative human value.

> [T]he globalizing field of the new phenomenon of the Western world system, a field whose origins lay in specific historical events and processes of cultural transformation, that had taken place in Europe; processes of transformation, whose epochal secularization of what it is like to be/not be human, in effect of human identity, was, however, to be gradually imposed on the rest of the peoples of the world.[35]

Wynter's outline creates the space to color in how the aforementioned Western cultural transformation intersects with race and contributes to the gradation of human value, which Chen explores on the animacy scale. Wynter writes, "Western Humanism's two secular sociogenic codes enacting of each form of *Man* (as the incarnation of symbolic *life*), and the Human Others (as the embodiment of symbolic *death*), as codes therefore, to which we give the ethno-taxonomic term of *race*, since they, and which, can be logically enacted only on the basis of the West's negation of equal co-humanness."[36] The expanse between "symbolic life" and "symbolic death" (and their racial representatives) is imbricated with Chen's understanding of the animacy scale and its levels of aliveness. Wynter argues that, through sociohistorical and cultural processes, White male subjects (Man) made themselves signifiers of human life itself, and, as a result, the value of all other forms of life must be ascertained vis-à-vis their relative positioning to this symbolic life.

For Chen, language, in the form of defining, insulting, and shaming, is a technology employed to map racialized matter on the animacy scale. "[I]f animacy gradations have linguistic consequences and linguistic consequences are also always political ones, then animacy gradations are inextricably political."[37] Positioning Black and Brown subjects, Black and Brown racialized matter, at the bottom of the human animacy hierarchy is a political act. This political positioning has been, and is being, accomplished, in part, by subjects at the top of the hierarchy using political power to define Black and Brown subjects as less than human—as "approaching animality." Reading Marx's understanding of capitalism's impact on disenfranchised subjects, Chen writes, "[H]uman animality (barbarity) represents the simultaneous legitimation of enslavement, a relative lack of philosophical awareness other than recognition of one's need to be ruled, and a dispossession of right to self-determination (hence, justified enslavement)."[38]

When subjects at the top the human hierarchy are able to define subjects at the bottom as less than human, as approaching animality, it allows less than human treatment toward bottom dwellers to be normalized; it allows State-sponsored violence against unarmed Black and Brown citizens to be normalized until it becomes unpunishable, as in the cases of Michael Brown and Eric Garner. A similarly troubling negative externality of State-sponsored violence against unarmed Black and Brown citizens is that it contributes to an environment where non-State-sponsored violence against these citizens can go unpunished, as in the case of Trayvon Martin. The State sets the sociopolitical and juridical mapping for moving Black and Brown subjects toward bare life; subjects of the State (including, at times, Black and Brown subjects) follow the road map to assist in moving Black and Brown subjects toward bare life.

The who, why, and how of bare life directional movement will be critical throughout this discussion. Both Chen and Bennett investigate how movement intersects with power and matter, and how power and matter are mapped on animacy hierarchies. Bennett borrows Bruno Latour's term, actant, to activate her analysis. "An actant is a source of action that can be either human or non-human; it is that which has efficacy, can do things, has sufficient coherence to make a difference, produce effects, alter the course of events. It is 'any entity that modifies another entity in a trial'; something whose 'competence is deduced from its performance' rather than posited in advance of the action."[39] As an action source, entity modifier, and effect producer, an actant literally moves matter.

With her vibrant matter discussion and "thing-power" concept, Bennett expands on Latour's actant notion by adding and highlighting affect: the movement of emotions. Bennett avers, "The notion of thing-power aims instead to attend to the it in actant . . . since things do in fact affect other bodies, enhancing and weakening their power."[40] Chen, too, highlights affect in her reading of Latour but accentuates affect's potential to move multiple bodies at once, a perspective that this argument will explore later. Chen writes, "I define affect without necessary restriction, that is, I include the notion that affect is not something necessarily corporeal and that it potentially engages many bodies at once, rather than (only) being contained as an emotion within a single body. Affect inheres in the capacity to affect and be affected. Yet I am also interested in the relatively subjective, individually held 'emotion' or 'feeling.'"[41] Chen would likely be interested in Anzaldúa's relatively subjective and individually held affect, because it is rooted in animating personal and societal change. Anzaldúa writes about animating her creative process:

> My 'awakened dreams' are about shifts. Thought shifts, reality shifts, gender shifts . . . I am playing with my Self, I am playing with the world's soul, I am in dialogue between my Self and *el espíritu del mundo*. I change myself, I change the world. Sometimes I put my imagination to a more rare use. I choose words, images, and body sensations and animate them on my consciousness, thereby making changes in my belief system.[42]

Anzaldúa and Chen are concerned with the relationship between affect and animacy, especially as it relates to increasing agency in racialized embodied matter.

Bennett and Chen's interventions into the relationships between matter, animacy, actants, and affect allows us to return to the concern raised by Ziarek: whether bare life, itself, can be mobilized by emancipatory movements. White male subjects, as inhabitants at the top of the animacy hierarchy in the United States, have the most potential to operate as powerful actants. Historically and contemporaneously, White males in the United States have had the most power to effect and affect other American subjects along the animacy hierarchy—including other White male subjects.[43] Historically, White male subjects, as juridical agents and the primary creators of juridical structures, have powerfully effected how American racialized subjects interface with the legal system. White male subjects, for example, legally institutionalized a system of forced servitude, whereby Black subjects were sold as labor and had no legal claim over the rights of their bodies. The affect of chattel slavery on some Black subjects involved debilitating depression, severe shame and self-destructive self-loathing.[44] In the following chapter, Hortense Spillers argues that these slavery-tethered markings can be passed down through generations. However, the Black Radical Tradition documents a history of agentic, ontological defining resistance to anti-Black violence inclusive of New York City's 1712 slave revolt, Stono, South Carolina's slave uprising in 1739, the Nat Turner-led Southhampton Insurrection in 1831, the 1890s crystallization of the Anti-Lynching Movement in which Ida B. Wells featured prominently, the Watts Uprising in 1965, and the formation of the Black Lives Matter Movement in 2013.[45]

In the context of the aforementioned oppressive, sociopolitical and juridical history, animating Black and Brown subjects toward liberatory action is a challenge that necessitates effective organizing and an embrace of aesthetics, affect, and ethics. While acknowledging the unpredictable and indeterminate nature of the aesthetics-affect-ethical relationship, Bennett suggests that this relationship, when linked to exemplary stories, can fire subjects' imaginations and move bodies into action:

> One can begin by acknowledging that there is no way to guarantee that an aesthetic disposition will produce or even incline toward goodness, generosity, or social justice. Affect can join narcissism, beauty can serve violence, and enchantment can foster cruelty . . . There are, however, some positive ways to respond to the ethical indeterminacy

of affect, though here, too, no cure exists. One can, for example, argue on behalf of a particular ethical use of affect or, in, what is perhaps, a more effective strategy, tell exemplary stories of such uses in the hope of enchanting bodies and inflecting imaginations towards them."[46]

Bennett is correct and prudent in addressing the unpredictable and indeterminate nature of the aesthetics-affect-ethical relationship. This study will acknowledge these affect-related concerns while reading "exemplary stories" in American literatures that illuminate liberatory technologies. *Animating Black and Brown Liberation* will argue that an embrace of aesthetics, in the form of exemplary narratives, can help move Black, Brown, and other marginalized subjects into emancipatory action by serving as a repository for liberatory strategies and best practices. The project avers that novels, plays, and poems qua matter are actants, which can affect human matter enough to move human matter into liberatory action. Discussing his Black spatial imaginary[47] notion, George Lipsitz's analysis coheres with the art qua matter liberatory approach: "[E]xpressive culture contest[s] the oppressions of race by imagining strategic realignments of place, by presenting strategies for altering scale, scope, and stakes of space—for burrowing in building up, and branching out. They proceed from a philosophy that sees art as a vital part of life of a community."[48]

Animating Black and Brown Liberation will argue that Black and Brown socially-engaged cultural producers (liberatory novelists, playwrights, and poets) are also actants. These cultural producers' subject positions as Black and Brown artists places pressure on the idea that subjects positioned at the bottom of the human animacy scale have relatively little power to effect and affect subjects on the animacy scale above them. While acknowledging the problematics involved in "romanticizing" the artist, this study will demonstrate that some activist-oriented artists have the ability to affect individuals and groups enough to animate them into ethical, social justice-related, emancipatory action. Socially-engaged artists have the affective power to move individuals and groups to think deeply about injustice's moral underpinnings and help move these same individuals and groups from thought to action—from thought to "*doing* good."

Reading Kant's analysis of moral motivation, Bennett writes:

> [M]oral motivation involves the power that [Kant] attributes to moral exemplars and archetypes. These ideal, true forms have a kind of centripetal force that draws humans in their vicinity into their orbit; they infect free beings and induce conduct resembling that of the exemplar or archetype.[49]

Socially-engaged Black and Brown artists are not necessarily "moral exemplars" but their activist orientation, access to public platforms to express their art, and general commitment to social justice can signify a desire to "*do good*"[50] for their respective communities; these socially-engaged artists can "infect free beings" among the folk, while performing an inspirational, community healer role. *Animating Black and Brown Liberation* will examine American literatures, featuring socially-engaged Black and Brown artist-activist-healer-oriented characters, who are endeavoring to move community members toward emancipatory thought and action; the study will analyze how these characters draw Black and Brown subjects "in their vicinity into their orbit" and "infect" them with a desire to engage in conduct resembling that of an artist-activist-healer—which is to say, infect them with a desire to do good.

This project is also interested in understanding how an artist's ability to move liberatory ideas into liberatory action can infect a critical mass of Black and Brown subjects, so that these subjects will be inspired to co-create a "movement" of people working to turn liberatory ideas into liberatory action. Aligning with Chen's reading that affect "potentially engages many bodies at once," *Animating Black and Brown Liberation* avers that individual socially-engaged Black and Brown artists, creating alone, or in concert with other artists, have the potential to affect many bodies at once, helping to animate a liberatory movement. Using African-American narratives, in particular, is a productive approach to study how Black and Brown socially-engaged artists perform leadership roles in emancipatory movements, because the State's juridical and sociopolitical disenfranchisement of African Americans (including restrictive housing covenants, employment restrictions, mass incarceration, et al.) established a model for the State's disenfranchisement of Latinx communities and other American marginalized communities. Erica R. Edwards argues, "[T]wentieth and early twenty-first-century African-American narrative has been a site of discursive struggle whereby ideals of Black leadership have been both made and unmade, post-civil rights Black fiction and film have often forged political contestation through the formal achievement of *curiosity*: a politics and aesthetics of serious interrogation, playful questioning, thoughtful puzzling, and fantastic reinvention."[51]

African-American author Toni Cade Bambara's *The Salt Eaters* and Latinx author Salvador Plascencia's *The People of Paper* are both liberatory literary narratives marked by serious interrogation, playful questioning, and fantastic reinvention. *The Salt Eaters*, a novel published in 1980 at the dawning of American neoliberalism's rise to pervasive influence, is cultural labor that chronicles Black (and people of color) community activists struggling to develop and implement discursive best practices to help their fracturing communities resist hegemonic State pressures. *The People of Paper*, published in 2005 near the apex of American neoliberalism's rise, is a novel that examines the ways in which Latinx subjects seek liberation from the hegemonic gaze of a disciplining, mysterious, force in the sky. Aihwa Ong understands neoliberalism as a construct that introduces a market-based rationale to a brand of governance that is disciplinary and is rooted in the notion of optimization.[52] Specifically, Ong asserts that the American form of neoliberalism (the most pervasive and most frequently exported model) is a "market rationality that promotes individualism and entrepreneurism that engenders debates about the norms of citizenship and the value of human life."[53] For Timothy Brennan, along with the goal of dismantling the welfare state, "neoliberalism argues that an unrestrained market logic, freed from governmental restraints, will cure social ills and lead to general prosperity."[54] David Harvey maintains, "Neoliberalism is, in the first instance, a theory of political and economic practices that proposes that human well-being can be advanced by liberating individual entrepreneurial freedoms and skills within a[n] institutional framework characterized by strong private property rights, free markets and free trade."[55]

If neoliberalism can be understood as a vulgar embrace of human commodification masquerading as a liberatory economic technology, then Plascencia's and Bambara's novels can be understood as cultural labor that unmasks human commodification masquerading as a liberatory economic technology. In these novels, ankhing animates Black and Brown liberation within neoliberal-era artistic counterpublics, by employing Spirit as an actant to resist State-sponsored hegemony towards Black and Brown subjects. Ankhing can be defined as a process in sociopolitical and economic struggle, whereby individuals and groups organize themselves to resist hegemonic forces, which seek to delimit their subjectivity, their social, political and economic agency, and their power to determine their own life courses.[56]

Ankhing and the Spirit

In this study, the Egyptian ankh functions as an indigenous spiritual representation of animacy. In Kemetic (ancient Egyptian) traditional spiritual cosmology, the ankh represents "life, to live, living."[57] The ankh has a generative relationship to this project's understanding of animacy (a quality of agency, awareness, mobility, and aliveness). The understanding of the ankh as animacy is critical because it underscores the agency and mobility of this indigenous African spiritual technology. Ankh qua animacy is particularly productive in a study that examines Black and Brown liberatory agency, and is mindful of Ziarek's concern: "Whether bare life itself can be mobilized by emancipatory movements." The action, movement, and affect that the ankhing gerund signifies, is the action, movement, and affect that animates sociopolitical movements. Ankhing builds upon and reinvents action, movement, and affect in the context of liberatory communal labor: men and women meet in counterpublics to enhance life for themselves and others via animating emancipatory, Spirit-infused movements. During the aforementioned processes, ankhing operates as an actant, a "source of action that can be either human or non-human; it is that which has efficacy, can do things, has sufficient coherence to make a difference, produce effects, alter the course of events."

Social justice is the goal of Bambara's and Plascencia's ankhing-tethered, fictional, sociopolitical movements. Molefi Kete Asante links the ankh to the Kemetic notion "maat," an ethics-related concept that values living a life rooted in justice,[58] and to the ancient Malian notion "nommo," the animating power of the spoken word.[59] In *The Salt Eaters* and *The People of Paper*, nommo breathes life, breathes Spirit, into social justice work during the ankhing process.

The etymological origin of the word "spirit" includes the Latin "spirare," which translates as "to breathe."[60] Spirit is breath, and speech, and song; Spirit's expression signifies that life is indwelling and, with each exhalation, the Spirit hails to all present: "recognize—I am." This call for recognition is both power play and power trap. Spirit's self-hailing is a power play, because it is a declaration of identity, an establishing of subjectivity in the world of phenomena; Spirit's self-hailing is a power trap, because it is a call for recognition, in the context of unequal power relations, which leaves the relatively less powerful caller at the mercy of the relatively more powerful receiver—who may choose not to recognize a racialized caller. Franz Fanon argues:

> Man is human only to the extent to which he tries to impose himself on another man in order to be recognized by him. As long as he has not been recognized by the other, it is this other who remains the focus of his actions. His human work and reality depend on this other and on his recognition by the other. It is in this other that the meaning of life is condensed. There is no open conflict between White and Black. One day the White master recognized without struggle the black slave. But the former slave wants to have himself recognized . . . It is when I go beyond my immediate existential being that I apprehend the being of the other as a natural reality, and more than that. If I shut off the circuit, I make the two-way movement unachievable, I keep the other within himself. In an extreme degree, I deprive him even of this being-for-self.[61]

Resistance to this lack of recognition, resistance to this deprivation of being-for-self, necessitates a breath, a speech act, a song of resistance. Sometimes the song is a shout or a shriek because that is all that Spirit, all that breath, can produce when responding to dehumanizing forces. Dehumanizing forces are the hegemonic forces that seek to rob the body of life and Spirit—forces that try to give the Spirit the blues.

In *The Spirituals & the Blues*,[62] James H. Cone, whose foundational work in liberation theology connects Black freedom possibilities to sociocultural institutions accessible to working-class Black folks, argues that African-American spirituals and their secular progeny, the blues, are critical liberatory cultural productions of the Black expressive culture tradition. Cone posits that "Black Spirit" is the power source of Black spirituals and the blues.[63] Cone sets the context for his definition of

Black Spirit by first sharing his spiritual hush harbor[64] experience of growing up in a Black church in Bearden, Arkansas.

> At Macedonia A.M.E. Church, the Spirit of God was no abstract, no vague perception of philosophical speculation. The Spirit was the 'power of God unto salvation,' that 'wheel in the middle of the wheel.' The Spirit was God himself breaking into the lives of the people, 'building them up where they were torn down and proppin' them up on every leanin' side.' The Spirit was God's presence with the people and his will to provide them the courage and strength to make it through.[65]

Although Cone is, specifically, defining the "the Spirit of God" (and not the "Black Spirit"), he is suggesting that the two notions are imbricated. Cone is implying that the "Spirit that was God's presence with the people" is the Black Spirit, and suggesting that the Black artists, the Black spirituals singers who helped to bring the Black Spirit to Macedonia A.M.E.'s parishioners, were able to do so because that same Black Spirit was *in* the Black spirituals singers. Cone argues that as a result of this Black Spirit presence, the singers were able to invoke the Black Spirit throughout the congregation, like a dialectical contagion that spreads the weary blues, while simultaneously serving as a liberatory blues vaccine. This blues vaccine, this collective spiritual healing as resistance, is an articulation of Clyde Woods's blues epistemology notion that "involves the constant reestablishment of collective sensibility in the face of constant attacks."[66]

The Spirit resists constant attacks by the State's biopower, the State's ability to make live and let die;[67] Spirit rejects social death[68] as it embraces Black becoming. The holy shout, yell, and scream announce, "I'm alive." This spiritual dialectic between artist and community creates a unity that can be placed in the service of collectivist emancipatory labor inside and outside hush harbor walls:

> 'Have mercy, please.' This cry is not a cry of passivity, but a faithful, free response to the movement of the Black Spirit. It is the movement of the Black Spirit. It is the black community accepting themselves as the people of the Black Spirit and knowing through his presence

> that no chains can hold the Spirit of Black humanity in bondage . . . Black music is unity music. It unites the joy and the sorrow, the love and the hate, the hope and the despair of black people; and it moves the people toward the direction of total liberation.[69]

"Have mercy, please," the speech act operating as moan and lyric, is a public acknowledgment of immense discomfort. This moan/lyric is a blues lament inoculating fellow blues people. In the blues epistemology[70] context, Woods writes, "Born in an era of censorship, suppression, and persecution, the blues conveyed the sorrow of the individual and collective tragedy that had befallen African Americans."[71] Shared epistemic sorrows visited upon racialized Black subjects animates Black Spirit's conductivity in the communal space. Experiential blues knowledge, blues epistemology, allows the Black Spirit to pass from person-to-person in a hush harbor Black church, or pass from person-to-person in a hush harbor Black cultural center. This transference can occur during artistic performance. The Spirit can pass from ancestor to person (when invoked by a speech act, operating as a moan/lyric) where, as Fred Moten asserts "shriek turns speech turns song."[72]

However, Cone makes access to this dialectic transference restrictive. Cone makes the essentialist argument that "it is not possible to render an authentic interpretation of Black music without having shared and participated in the black experience that created it. Black music must be *lived* before it can be understood . . . And that experience is available only to those who share the *Spirit* and participate in the *faith* of the people who created these songs."[73] Certainly, the specific, racialized experience of a Black subject (whose ancestors began their sojourn in North America as Black objects, as property, as capital) is likely to have unique insight into the meaning and Spirit of spirituals and the blues. However, relatively low melanin levels do not occlude the Spirit from entering into a non-melaninized subject, especially when that non-Black subject has experienced their own specific type of blues. It is possible that a White, transgender whistle-blower, who had been imprisoned for revealing State secrets (that State citizens have a right to know), probably understands enough about the blues to moan her way through 16 bars until shriek turns speech turns song.

The blues' powerful artistic beauty (and the Black Spirit's powerful artistic beauty that animates the blues) has the potential to liberate

Black subjects; Black Spirit is informed by nature, by embodied experience, but it is not confined by nature, by racialized phenomena: the epidermis cannot prevent the blues from doing what the blues do. This cultural production has the potential to liberate a subject who has known significant subjugation and is willing to let the powerful, emancipatory Spirit of art have its way. While remaining aware of G. W. F. Hegel's aesthetic and philosophical racism,[74] his insight into the intersection of art, Spirit, and liberation is productive:

> For the beauty of Art, is beauty that is born and born again of the Spirit; and as the Spirit and its productions stands higher than nature with her phenomena, so does also the beauty of Art stand higher than the beauty of nature . . . for in such a fancy there is involved both spirituality and freedom.[75]

It is this spirituality and freedom, the spiritual and the political, that the ankhing process seeks to honor, cultivate, and use as liberatory technologies in artistic counterpublics. Ankhing technologies embrace the power of the sensorium. In the ankhing process, feeling and the rational are not strange bedfellows; they are embodied bedsisters. Audre Lorde argues:

> There are many kinds of power, used and unused, acknowledged or otherwise. The erotic is a resource within each of us that lies in a deeply female and spiritual plane, firmly rooted in the power of our unexpressed or unrecognized feeling . . . [I]t has become fashionable to separate the spiritual (psychic and emotional) from the political, to see them as contradictory or antithetical. 'What do you mean, a poetic revolutionary, a meditating gunrunner?' In the same way, we have attempted to separate the spiritual and the erotic . . . The dichotomy between the spiritual and the political is also false, resulting from an incomplete attention to our erotic knowledge.[76]

Lorde is interrogating masculinist modalities of power and advocating for a more expansive, gendered subjectivity that is open to the use of "what is deepest and strongest and richest within each of us, being shared: the passions of love, in its deepest meanings."[77]

Building upon Lorde, erotic power is erotic energy, erotic vibration. This vibration can be transformed into liberatory motion, liberatory movements. The aforementioned transformation was on display at Vibrations during that warm, August night in Inglewood, California, described in this chapter's opening. The social justice passions in a crowded room of articulate, committed activists exchanging ideas and exchanging energy, engendered a palpable eroticism to the proceedings. In physics, the Law of Conservation of Energy states that energy cannot be created or destroyed, instead, it only changes forms or is transferred from one object to another.[78] Yet, in this transference, a percentage of heat and energy is lost. Although not writing in scientific terms, when Lorde suggests transferring erotic energy to liberation energy, she does not reference the energy lost, the slippage, during the exhausting organizing work that *is* freedom work. This slippage is why artistic counterpublics like Vibrations are so critical; they are venues where like-minded activists can re-energize, regain lost energy and regenerate the life force necessary to maintain effective engagement in liberatory labor. Paradoxically, in the revivifying exchange of erotically-charged, liberation energy, some emancipatory passion is lost in the fire.

Coterminous with Lorde's understanding of erotic power, the power propelling ankhing technologies in Vibrations-like artistic counterpublics is often suspicious of rigid hierarchies, though not immune to them. Ankhing-tethered processes have an epistemological openness (though not replete) to non-patriarchal leadership modalities, a respect for generative, communal labor, and a battered weariness from what Erica R. Edwards calls the "violences of charisma,"[79] which emanates from "one of the central fictions of black American politics: that freedom is best achieved under the direction of a single charismatic leader."[80] Echoing Edwards, the ankhing process resists the Great Man approach to community liberation and embraces an emancipatory communal labor approach.

Although the ankh (and ankhing by association) is a productive technology to employ given the subject, direction, and scope of this project, it can be argued that the icon's use is problematic due to its connection to 1960s through 1990s-era Black Nationalism/Afrocentrism, which, at times, embraced misogyny, homophobia, and narrow, exclusionary Black essentialism. In the context of virulent

1960s-through-1990s-era anti-Blackness and a long tradition of non-Africans demonizing Africa, African culture, history and progeny, some emancipatory-oriented African Americans looked to reclaim and embrace Africa by reclaiming outward expressions of "Africaness," (i.e., dashikis, braids, afros) and African iconography, including the ankh. However, the reclamation project was too often rooted in romantic, simplistic notions that privileged men, masculinist ideas, and male folkways, while marginalizing women, their ideas, and their folkways. As a complement to the hyper-masculinity, the African reclamation project, at times, included a hyper-homophobia that aggressively demonized same-gendered lovers as "unnatural," "un-African" White-minded traitors to the race.[81]

During this Black Nationalist/Afrocentric era, a series of effective feminist and queer critiques emerged to address the aforementioned misogyny and homophobia. In "Double Jeopardy: To Be Black and Female," Frances Beale writes in the foundational *The Black Woman*, "Those who are exerting their 'manhood' by telling Black women to step back into a domestic, submissive role are assuming a counter-revolutionary position. Black women likewise have been abused by the system and we must begin talking about the elimination of all kinds of oppression."[82] Writing in the same anthology, which she edited, Toni Cade Bambara argues, "[The Black woman] is being assigned an unreal role of mute servant that supposedly neutralizes the acidic tension that exists between Black men and Black women. She is being encouraged—in the name of the revolution no less—to cultivate 'virtues' that if listed would sound like the personality traits of slaves."[83]

Critic and activist Barbara Smith, who was active in the Civil Rights, Black Liberation, Women's Rights, and Gay Rights Movements, opines about the interlocking nature of racism, misogyny, and homophobia, "Black power activists and Black nationalists generally viewed lesbians and gay men anathema—White-minded traitors to the race . . . Because I came out in the context of the Black liberation, women's liberation, and—most significantly—the newly emerging Black feminist movement that I was helping to build, I worked from the assumption that all of the 'isms' were connected."[84]

Jean Bond and Patricía Peery write about the aggressive attacks that Black women endured from Black men—in the name of Black Nationalist revolution:

> For their part, many Black men berate Black women for their faults, faults so numerous and so pronounced that one is hard put to discern in their tirade, any ground, short of invisibility, on which Black womanhood may redeem itself. They do this, blind to the age-old implications of such a vociferous rejection of a part of themselves. Others run on about the necessity of subordinating women to their superior and manly will in the planning and execution of revolution.[85]

Sharon Patricia Holland argues that the genealogy of these intra-community attacks and connected "isms" can be traced to religious institutions and ideologies that claim to be "pro-Black," but whose "pro-Blackness" morphs into "anti-Blackness" when referencing Black gay community members. Responding to Ron Simmons's essay, "Some Thoughts on the Challenges Facing Black Gay Intellectuals," Holland concurs that there is great deal of homophobia in pro-Black organizations like the traditional Black Church and the Nation of Islam, and that some religious leaders within these organizations "equate 'homosexuality and adultery with rape and child molestation' and interpret religious and critical texts to fit this equation."[86]

Given the aforementioned queer and feminist critiques, and the voluminous number of unmentioned queer and feminist critiques,[87] why employ the ankh in this emancipatory-centered study? While acknowledging these critiques (and the fact that the ankh itself is not a stand-in for homophobia or misogyny) there remain useful concepts associated with the ankh in its use as a theoretical and methodological lens. This study is utilizing the ankh, because the ankh is too valuable as a spiritual technology, historical artifact, and Black cultural touchstone to be dismissed due to problematic symbolic associations over the last 50 years—especially when it has been a transformative animating force for over 5,000 years. In some ways, this study is an ankh recovery project. In a Kemetian spiritual approach to meditation, the ankh (along with other ancient Egyptian iconography) plays a central role. While using extremely deep breathing to reduce the breath count and slow the heart rate, which facilitates access to the trance state, the practitioner visualizes the ankh (often paired with other icons in the spiritual system) moving through their body as a healing modality or the practitioner visualizes holding the ankh in their hand as a way to "bring into their possession" the qualities that the ankh and the other held icons represent.[88] Historically, the ankh has been a technology of healing and self-liberation, which are critical pieces to community liberation—and why the ankh is worth recovering.

Ankhing in Space

It may be productive to summarize a series of defining elements that ankhing includes and expand upon the nomenclature found in these defining elements. (1) Ankhing is a process in sociopolitical and economic struggle, whereby individuals and groups organize themselves to resist hegemonic forces, which seek to delimit their subjectivity, social, political and economic agency, and delimit their power to determine their own life courses. (2) Ankhing is a process in sociopolitical and economic struggle, whereby inspiration, strategy, and communal labor comingle to serve the aforementioned subjects in their efforts to collectively think through the most effective means to resist hegemonic forces—and through this idea-exchange, inspire, motivate, and move each other toward best practices to resist hegemonic forces seeking to delimit their subjectivity, social, political, and economic agency, and delimit their power to determine their own life courses. This process includes rigorous self-interrogation and group interrogation toward creating a healthy, whole, ankhing process that can result in healthy, whole, ankhing practices and outcomes.

Though not speaking specifically about ankhing, Moraga offers insight into the efficacy of self- and group-interrogation: "In Toni Cade Bambara's novel *The Salt Eaters*, the Black curandera asks the question, 'Can you afford to be whole?' This line represents the question that has burned within me for years and years through my growing politicization. What would a movement bent on the freedom of women of color look like? In other words what are the implications of looking not only outside of our culture but into our culture and ourselves and from that place beginning to develop a strategy for a movement that could challenge the bedrock of oppressive systems of belief globally."[89] (3) Ankhing desires to animate and nurture nascent sociopolitical and economic empowerment movements by embracing the erotic, the spiritual, and other sensorium-tethered epistemes. This sensorium-embrace can produce a generative, liberatory power to start, nurture, and sustain individuals and groups in their efforts to organize and move in the direction of freedom. (4) Ankhing privileges alterity, diverse ideas, democratic decision-making, and concomitant communal labor to implement democratically agreed upon courses of action, while explicitly rejecting the tired tradition of patriarchal, Great Man, top-down leadership-style that has historically marked racialized emancipatory organizing labor.[90]

The preceding enhanced definition of ankhing is an appropriate segue into a spatial intervention. There is a symbiotic and dialectical relationship between the ankhing process and the site where the ankhing process takes place. In *The Structural Transformation of the Public Sphere*,[91] Jürgen Habermas's investigation of the history, the workings, and the changing dynamics of the eighteenth- and nineteenth-century European (England, Germany, and France) bourgeois public sphere, he begins his study by discussing that "public," as it relates to physical buildings, does not necessarily mean that all citizens have access to these structures and the power they possess. "[I]n the expression, 'public building,' the term need not refer to general accessibility; the building does not even have to be open to the public traffic. 'Public buildings' simply house state institutions and as such are 'public.' The state is the 'public authority.' It owes this attribute to its tasks of promoting the public or common welfare of its rightful members."[92] In the United States, people of color subjects share a history marked by juridical, social, political, and economic maneuvers by the State to deny or limit their access to the public sphere. This State-sponsored circumscription signifies that, specifically, Brown and Black subjects are not "rightful" members of the State, despite their nominal status as United States citizens.

The aforementioned "wrongness" of Brown and Black citizens (in relation to denied access to full State membership and denied access to the often exclusionary bourgeois public happening in salons and coffeehouses where primarily White male private citizens met as intellectual equals to discuss and debate oppositional ideas[93]) necessitated the creation of alternative public spheres by these "wrong citizens." Nancy Fraser argues:

> [M]embers of subordinated social groups—women, workers peoples of color, gays and lesbians—have repeatedly found it advantageous to constitute alternative publics. I propose to

call these *subaltern counterpublics* in order to signal that they are parallel discursive arenas where members of subordinated social groups invent and circulate counterdiscourses which in turn permit them to formulate oppositional interpretations of their identities, interests and needs."[94]

Laura Pulido's research on the Mexican immigrant alternative public Centro de Acción Social Autónomo (CASA) is generative, because this subaltern counterpublic served as a site to circulate counterdiscourses for undocumented immigrant workers—an extreme representation of subjects perceived to be "wrong citizens." Founded in 1968 by Bert Corona, Chloe Alatorre, and the Mexican American Political Association, CASA was "part *mutualista* (mutual aid society for working class Mexicans), part social service organization, and part legal defense center—geared to Mexican immigrants."[95] CASA resisted the discourses that positioned undocumented immigrants inside the shadows and outside the boundaries of societal rights. This oppositional interpretation of undocumented immigrants' societal rights was evidenced in CASA's official list of demands, which included, "The total recognition of democratic rights of undocumented people."[96] These demands were not always embraced by some Latinx organizers who claimed undocumented workers undermined working class Mexican citizens by serving as strike breakers and, generally, serving as economic competition.[97] As a result, CASA was a counterpublic serving a marginalized group within a marginalized group.

Fraser speaks of a counterpublic to counter the counterpublic: a space where historically disenfranchised subjects can address the experience of being marginalized *within* the opposition. Fraser rightly sees the need for counterpublics like CASA and Vibrations to help subordinated peoples "formulate oppositional interpretations of their identities, interests and needs." Maylei Blackwell, signaling the import of Chicana feminist counterpublic oppositional memories qua oral histories, writes, "Re-membering is a vital act in creating political subjectivity, and Chicana feminists . . . strategies include re-membering themselves in time and place, being whole under erasure, creating new terrains of memory . . . Oral history is part of this repertoire of remembrance and shares a political tradition with Latin American *testimonio*."[98] Catherine R. Squires suggests that enclaves are possible sites to cultivate and transform memories into discursive strategies:

"Marginalized groups are commonly denied public voice or entrance into public spaces by dominant groups and thus are forced into enclaves. At different times in history, African Americans and Latinx subjects have been forced into enclaves by repressive State policies and have used these enclave spaces to create discursive strategies and gather oppositional resources . . . [A]n enclave public sphere requires the maintenance of safe spaces."[99]

The maintenance of safe spaces is essential in the ankhing process, which includes the process whereby inspiration, strategy, and communal labor comingle to animate and nurture nascent sociopolitical and economic empowerment movements, via employing evolving democratic, non-patriarchal, Spirit-infused technologies. Physical, intellectual, emotional, spiritual, gender, racial, and sexual-orientation-based modes of safety are essential for empowering diverse subjects to speak, think, and strategize freely in the communal effort to gather oppositional resources. Embracing diverse subject positions, within the confines of a counterpublic, is an oppositional resource. Inclusivity and the acknowledgment that epistemological labor can be generated from subjugated subjects *inside* a subjugated group, resists the troubling phenomena of oppressed subjects mimicking their oppressors. Embracing counterpublic inclusivity resists the counterpublic becoming *counter* to the counterpublic.

It may be productive to offer an expanded series of counterpublic characteristics. Squires's generative understanding of the counterpublic involves:

> Spaces and discourses: protest rhetoric; persuasion; increased interpublic communication and interaction with the state; occupation and reclamation of the dominant and state-controlled public spaces; strategic use of enclave spaces . . . Goals: foster resistance; test arguments and strategies in wider publics; create alliances; persuade outsiders to change views; perform public resistance to oppressive laws and social codes; gain allies . . . Sanctions: threat of violence, disrespect, or dismissal from dominant publics and state; co-optation of counterpublicity.[100]

Squires focuses on the resistance element of the counterpublic by identifying as counterpublic characteristics: "protest rhetoric," "foster resistance," and "perform public resistance to oppressive laws and social codes." For some subjugated subjects, subjects whose material conditions are adversely impacted by State policies, resisting hegemonic and societal forces' negative impact upon their lifeworlds is a priority; for some subaltern citizens, lifting oppressive yokes is priority enough to move them toward counterpublics for solidarity with fellow oppressed citizens and solidarity with fellow communal laborers committed to developing and implementing strategic liberatory actions. Squires privileges intra-counterpublic and inter-counterpublic communication, because the latter performs the crucial labor of producing allies and changing minds outside the group, while the former performs the equally critical labor of identifying best emancipatory practices and helping to negotiate the difficulties that a diverse group is likely to face under oppressive pressures.

Squires's listing of counterpublic characteristics can be expanded for several reasons. (1) Squires's counterpublic characteristics do not include a prioritization of intra-counterpublic evolution. Evolution is a critical component to a liberatory group because it needs to be nimble when facing a State's hegemonic powers. (2) Squires does not include Spirit as an element. (3) Squires does not include an explicit goal of transforming societies.

Animating Black and Brown Liberation expands Squires's counterpublic characteristics. Adding an "intra-counterpublic evolution" aspect promotes evolutionary self/group interrogation about how the self/group creates, develops, and adjudicates epistemological approaches and liberatory practices to respond to the State's hegemonic forces. This type of evolution is required, because emancipatory internal structures and emancipatory internal systems are not static—especially under a totalizing and atomizing neoliberal imperative. As a result, a counterpublic characteristic listing should include an evolutionary-related element, because without an evolutionary element, a counterpublic is in danger of becoming a space that *used to be* safe, or a space that used to have counterpublicity, or a space that simply used to be.

Second, counterpublic characteristics should include a Spirit-related term. At times, the Spirit is unrecognized (although present) in counterpublics, because Spirit does not hail itself; it does not call attention to itself. Spirit is embedded in the feeling. Spirit is the technology that can allow the dispossessed to feel good about themselves, their culture, and their community; Spirit can allow disenfranchised subjects to feel beautiful and valuable enough to resist oppression. As Cone asserts, Spirit is the generative power that literally "moves the people toward the direction of total liberation." A listing of counterpublic characteristics should include a Spirit element, because it is the people's elevated Spirit that can allow them to do the people's work of resisting inside—and eventually outside—the counterpublic.

Third, a listing of counterpublic characteristics should include a goal of transforming societies. Transformation of societies should be a goal on a list of counterpublic characteristics, because perpetual liberatory struggle is not a productive goal; it is a Sisyphusian curse. Perpetual struggle is physically, emotionally, and psychologically exhausting for even the most committed community laborer. There should be an end-game or burn-out is inevitable; not breathing is possible.

The addition of the aforementioned three elements to Squires's understanding of counterpublics creates a discursive bridge to Margaret Kohn's notion of heterotopias of resistance. Kohn argues that the heterotopia of resistance is "a real countersite that inverts and contests existing economic or social hierarchies. Its function is social transformation rather than escapism, containment, or denial. By challenging conventions of the dominant society, it can be an important locus of struggle against normalization."[101]

Kohn builds upon Michel Foucault's notion of the heterotopia. Foucault writes about heterotopias:

> There also exists, and this is probably true for all cultures and civilizations, real and effective spaces which are outlined in the very institution of society, but which constitute a sort of counter-arrangement, of effectively realized utopia, in which all real arrangements that can be found within society, are at one and the same represented, challenged and overturned: a sort of place that lies outside all places and yet is localizable.[102]

Foucault's "counter-arrangement" is an arrangement in a space where resistance organizing, for example, can be effective. Resistance organizing can be effective at generating liberatory actions, while eschewing patriarchal approaches, while employing Spirit-based, power technologies, and while respecting and celebrating intra-counterspace subject diversity. Kohn rightly notes that Foucault does not claim that heterotopias are a tool of political emancipation and social transformation.[103]

Heterotopias of Resistance

In contradistinction to Foucault's heterotopias, Kohn's heterotopias of resistance are sites for political liberation and their "function is social transformation." Furthermore, Kohn argues that heterotopias of resistance are "sites that foster oppositional practices by sheltering counterhegemonic ideas and identities."[104] By "counterhegemonic ideas and identities," Kohn suggests that heterotopias of resistance are "safe havens" for ideas that privilege democratic-styles of information-sharing, decision-making, and communal labor, while functioning as safe havens for subjects (and their ideas), who may represent difference *within* heterotopias of resistance. Kohn suggests that alterity is not only acknowledged, but seen as a source of epistemological value and a resource for the effective implementation of collectively derived emancipatory strategies. Kohn asserts that heterotopias of resistance are "democratic. Their statues and by-laws establis[h] rules to guarantee both voting and deliberation; they set up procedures to ensure that everyone [can] speak and to prevent anyone from dominating the conversation . . . These sites mediat[e] individuals' identification with an oppositional political project—a political project motivated by diverse experiences."[105]

Kohn's heterotopias of resistance notion is also inclusive of the Spirit; the sensorium has a home in the "house of the people."[106] Kohn's research field for *Radical Space* are nineteenth- and early twentieth-century European heterotopias of resistance, some of which she hails as "houses of the people" that provided workers, socialists, and communists with safe havens to strategize, organize, and fight the hegemonic State forces. In 1899, after a house of the people's completion in Brussels, a poem was published on April 1, 1899, in the socialist newspaper *Le Peuple*.[107] In the poem, there is a clear acknowledgment of the generative role that Spirit plays in heterotopias of resistance:

> It is here, in this marvelous place
> That we will raise the battle cry
> It is here that ardor will awaken us
> And will make us remember fecund debates
>
> It is here that with words aflame
> Our representatives will come to speak to us
> Here that our souls will be sparked
> Here that we will find consolation

> It is here at the source of our study
> Full of ardor, we [illegible word]
> And it is here, connected to custom
> That we will come to fraternize.[108]

Given the mundane construction and unimaginative nomenclature, it is understandable why Kohn says the poem has "no literary merit,"[109] but it is significant that a *poem* was written and published in a socialist newspaper to commemorate the establishment of a heterotopia of resistance. It is significant that a Spirit-infused, cultural production was put in the service of a safe haven for political radicals and their supporters. Kohn writes, "The poem calls the house of the people 'the source of our study.' It is not merely a place where books, teachers and students come together; rather, something in the site itself provides a motivation for study . . . There is a reason to understand the workings of the social world because it is possible to change it. The poem also emphasizes the importance of place in encouraging emotional identification and motivating action. Words such as 'aflame,' 'pride,' 'ardor,' 'soul,' and 'spark' suggest that politics is about passion, and passion is more effectively captured by a material place than an abstract concept."[110]

Echoing Cone, Kohn argues that heterotopias of resistance are sites where liberatory subjects can "feel the Spirit."[111] In heterotopias of resistance, the Spirit is a technology used to encourage liberatory subjects' emotions, because emotion is a source of power. Liberatory subjects in heterotopias of resistance recognize, as Lorde does, that "[t]he dichotomy between the spiritual and the political is also false, resulting from an incomplete attention to our erotic knowledge."[112] Heterotopias of resistance make room for the uses of the erotic, because it is a democratic site that shelters "counterhegemonic ideas and identities";[113] it is a counterhegemonic site promoting the knowledge that feeling and the rational are not strange bedfellows, they are embodied bedsisters. As a result of the aforementioned qualities, heterotopias of resistance are the idea sites for the ankhing process: the process whereby inspiration, strategy, and communal labor comingle to animate and nurture nascent sociopolitical and economic empowerment movements, via employing evolving democratic, non-patriarchal, Spirit-infused technologies. The synergy between ankhing qualities and heterotopias of resistance qualities gives the ankhing process the best opportunity to produce the best practices for the liberation of subjugated peoples.

Artistic Heterotopias of Resistance

Toni Cade Bambara's *The Salt Eaters* chronicles activist artists trying to defend the collective humanity of their communities, so the novel is a productive space to start the interrogation of what this project calls "artistic heterotopias of resistance."[114] Building on the preceding heterotopias of resistance discussion, I will introduce *Animating Black and Brown Liberation*'s understanding of "artistic." Artistic refers to Spirit-infused cultural productions, the subjects who produce the cultural productions, and the concomitant sites where cultural productions are created. Artistic can also refer to a previously "non-artistic site" that has been transformed into an artistic site by the spontaneous creation of art, which is to say, that a non-artistic site can be improvisationally repurposed by cultural producers actively creating art "in the moment." In relationship to heterotopias of resistance, the primary function of the artistic is to "bring the Spirit" in greater measure and to enhance generative power in the service of emancipatory labor.

To set the context for the artistic heterotopias of resistance discussion in *The Salt Eaters* (briefly here, and fully in chapter 2), it may be productive to touch on "off-the-page" examples of groups with artistic heterotopias of resistance qualities. Throughout the twentieth and twenty-first centuries there have been American organizations that have had artistic heterotopias of resistance characteristics and featured artists in leadership roles. The 1930s-era League of Struggle for Negro Rights (the Communist Party's frontline organization in its outreach to African Americans) saw a role for artists in their social transformation agenda. Poet Langston Hughes was the League's president in 1934. The effusive Hughes promoted a collectivist, inclusive style of decision-making in the League, which certainly was a "safe haven" for "counterhegemonic ideas and identities," but ultimately the organization was vulnerable to the dictates of the top-down Communist Party.[115]

The Combahee River Collective contained more artistic heterotopia of resistance qualities than the League of Struggle for Negro Rights. The Combahee River Collective had its origins in the National

Black Feminist Organization. The National Black Feminist Organization was formed in August 1973 by Black feminists concerned that the Women Liberation Movement was not adequately dealing with race and class, and concerned that the Black Liberation Movement was not adequately dealing with sexism.[116] The first and only NBFO president Margaret Sloan explained that "by organizing around our needs as Black women, we are making sure that we won't be left out . . . which was what was appearing to be happening in both the Black Liberation and the Women Liberation Movements."[117]

As early as 1974, the Boston chapter of the NBFO began to organize themselves around a more explicitly anti-capitalist, socialist, and Black lesbian feminist agenda, eventually resulting in the formation of the Combahee River Collective.[118] In April 1977, the CRC published the Combahee River Collective Statement of definition, history, and intent. It became a foundational document in the establishment of strategic identity politics as a generative resistance tool. The statement reads in part:

> We are actively committed to struggling against racial, sexual, heterosexual, and class oppression and see as our particular task the development of integrated analysis and practice based upon the fact that major systems of oppression are interlocking. The synthesis of these oppressions creates the conditions of our lives. As Black women we see Black feminism as the logical political movement to combat the manifold and simultaneous oppressions that all women of color face.[119]

In the context of cultural production, Tiffany López argues that the process of how statements like the CRC Statement are created is as important as the statement itself. Process matters. After their initial exploratory meeting, the Combahee members began the process of self-definition and strategizing in a series of meetings that involved "an intense variety of consciousness raising"; they were intentional about having an inclusive, democratic, and non-hierarchical approach.[120] Combahee's approach aligns with ankhing, which is a process in sociopolitical and economic struggle, whereby inspiration, strategy, and communal labor comingle to help subjugated subjects collectively think through the most effective means to resist hegemonic forces.

Like Combahee's approach, ankhing's process includes rigorous self-interrogation and group interrogation toward creating healthy, emancipatory best practices and outcomes.

In Bambara's *The Salt Eaters*, an ankhing-related process makes artistic heterotopias of resistance safer and more productive, which is very similar to how ankhing-related practices worked with the Combahee River Collective. *The Salt Eaters* is a narrative that follows the lives of community activists with ties to the Feminist, Civil Rights, Black Power, Chicana/o Power, and Anti-War Movements. The narrative thrust is propelled by community activist Velma Henry who has recently attempted suicide by cutting her wrist and placing her head in a gas oven. At the start of the novel, Velma is under the care of a community healer, Minnie Ransom, who accesses traditional African religious healing modalities in her attempt to heal Velma. Velma resists the healing to such an extent that Minnie asks her, "Are you sure sweetheart that you want to be well?" This question also serves as the novel's opening line. In her work as a healer, Minnie is able to see and engage spiritual deities or "haints" from "the otherside." Minnie's spiritual guide, main helper, and primary interlocutor is a haint known as Old Wife. Old Wife is a spiritual deity who Minnie knew as a child when Old Wife was alive.

In *The Salt Eaters*, the relationship between Minnie and Old Wife can be read as a signifier for the unstable lives of racialized and gendered bodies that are committed to community spaces and community healing. While resisting hegemonic State forces, the healing labor expended in racialized communities can be exhausting, causing a slippage of energy. In oppressive contexts, healing whittles away at the healer; energy is lost, Spirit is lost during the transfer of wellness from community healer to wellness in the community in need. When alive, Old Wife was a community healer who gave to her community until she "gave up the ghost" and became a haint. Old Wife's haunting presence is Minnie's reminder of community healing's inherent dangers. The transfer of Spirit, of energy, from healer to community can result in anti-oppression labor becoming self-oppression labor. The cultural worker can labor till breathing becomes labored. A community activist can transfer her Spirit into nonexistence: she can heal to death. An activist can heal until she "ain't," heal until she becomes a haint. Instead of healing the community, the healer simply begins to haunt the community. Arthur Redding argues that "[H]aints, thus combines a distinct regional pronunciation of the word *haunts*, or ghosts, with the traditional corruption of *ain't*. Ghosts are haunt and ain't; ghosts are the nonexistent, the ain't, the other: They are both in the sense that they are immaterial or fugitive presences of the exiled and the abandoned."[121]

The Salt Eaters begins with Velma Henry in danger of becoming a haint. Velma the community activist and cultural worker has given away her energy, given away her breath, by sticking her head into an oven until she cannot breathe. Exhausted by healing activism, Velma relieves the State of its need to exercise biopower over her; she disciplines her own breath. This vulgar self-discipline animates the text's opening line, "Are you sure, Sweetheart, that you want to be well?" Minnie seeks surety from Velma because Minnie knows that the living have to consistently choose life—which often entails consistently choosing to enhance their level of animacy.

Methodology and How the Chapters Animate

This study's methodology is rooted in the literary arts (and not the Black Church or West African Dance, for example) because reading and writing—and the denial of reading and writing—perform outsized roles in African-American experiences vis-à-vis the State. When Frederick Douglass is taught reading and writing basics by Mrs. Auld, Mr. Auld (her husband and Douglass's slave master) forbids any further instruction, because it would forever "unfit [Douglass] to be a slave."[122] Mr. Auld's conviction about keeping Douglass illiterate provides Douglass with a revelation: "I now understood what had been to me a most perplexing difficulty—to wit, the White man's power to enslave the [Black people]. It was a grand achievement, and I prized it highly. From that moment I understood the pathway from slavery to freedom . . . I set out with the high hope, and a fixed purpose, at whatever cost of trouble, to learn how to read."[123] Douglass suggests that literacy acquisition can dramatically enhance a subject's animacy level; reading and writing can move a bare life individual from bondage to freedom. In *Animating Black and Brown Liberation*, ankhing is the liberatory technology employed to read American literatures *and* theorize ways to enhance animacy levels within the Latinx, African-American, and other disenfranchised communities. Facility with the literary arts is a generative means to move up the human animacy scale. In a liberatory study involving Black and Brown folk seeking heightened animacy in artistic counterpublics, the centering of literary arts is an essential move rooted in resistance. Edwards argues, "Literature is a repository for counter stories and alternative visions . . . narrative is a dialogic site for reimagining possibilities." Critically reading exemplary American literatures narratives, featuring effective, emancipatory-minded activists, can inspire effective, best practices to be utilized in real world liberatory labor.

The conflation of Spirit, animacy, and artistic counterpublic can produce a generative energy that helps to resist neoliberalism's hegemonic, atomizing forces on African-American and Latinx communities. Sociopolitically engaged Black and Brown artists operating in artistic counterpublics have the potential to facilitate liberatory resistance. Furthermore, this study contends that this artistically-rooted, liberatory labor is especially effective during sociopolitical struggle's ankhing-related process. The ankhing-related process in African-American and Latinx communities often takes place in Black and Brown emancipatory sites that, in many cases, would fall within rhetorician Vorris L. Nunley's definition of hush harbors: "Black publics [and, this study argues, Brown publics as well] where Black [and Brown] common sense, 'ideology lived and articulated in everyday understanding of the world and one's place in it,' is assumed to be hegemonic and normative."[124] Placing literary and cultural studies in conversations with theological and political theory produces a more replete understanding of what American literatures can teach us about liberation in disenfranchised American communities. Since African Americans and Latinx Americans share a history of State-sponsored juridical and socioeconomic oppression, [125] the emancipatory stories Black and Brown writers tell about themselves, and their respective communities, can provide insight into liberatory leadership strategies and discursive best practices for America's most vulnerable citizens to resist the State's oppressive forces.

Historically and concurrently, the State's oppressive forces, including State-sponsored racism, have been placed in the service of positioning White individuals at the top of the sociopolitical and economic hierarchy. Lipstiz argues, "[R]acism takes place in the United States not because of the irredeemably racist character of Whites as individuals, but because the racial project of Whiteness is so useful to elites as a mechanism for preserving hierarchy, exploitation and inequality in society at large."[126] In the American Imaginary, this inequality positions the perceived relative value of people of color—and their literatures—below the relative value of White Americans and their literature. Consequently, navigating the hierarchy, exploitation and inequality tethered to Whiteness is a major trope in the lived experiences of American people of color and a major trope in the American literatures of people of color. *Animating Black and Brown Liberation* focuses on African-American and Latinx literatures (while addressing Asian American and Native American literatures) to interrogate the liberatory possibilities of American literatures, featuring racialized subjects navigating hierarchy, exploitation, and inequality.

This project is divided into four chapters, each involving reading American literatures, while centering African-American and Latinx literatures. In chapter 1, Salvador Plascencia's *The People of Paper* is placed in conversation with Ishmael Reed's *Mumbo Jumbo*. Both novels are post-modernist narratives built around culturally-relevant, community-oriented, history-based mythologies. *The People of Paper* examines primarily Latinx and working-class El Monte, California's cultural history and interweaves this cultural history with a fictionalized, mytho-poetic world of a woman made of paper. *Mumbo Jumbo* mixes Kemetian mythology with Haitian mythology and historical figures from the Black Liberation Movement. Both texts are deeply interested in writing and literatures as ways to access liberation for racialized subjects.

In chapter 2, the project reads Bambara's *The Salt Eaters* in conjunction with Cherríe Moraga's play *Heroes and Saints*. These two narratives deal with the motivations, folkways, strategies, and challenges of people involved in emancipatory labor. Both stories feature activists whose troubled intimate relationships complicate their liberatory labor. The narratives explore environmental racism's impact on Black and Brown communities. *The Salt Eaters*'s protagonist Velma works as a computer programmer at a chemical plant. *Heroes and Saints* chronicles a farming community that is ravaged by chemical pesticide usage in the labor fields. Both narratives explore how the racialized body is devalued and debased in the neoliberal context.

Chapter 3 places the canon in conversation with two important anthologies that center women of color writers who are feminist activists. *This Bridge Called My Back: Writings by Radical Women of Color*, edited by Cherríe Moraga and Gloria Anzaldúa, and *June Jordan's Poetry for the People: A Revolutionary Blueprint*, edited by Lauren Muller and the Blueprint Collective are examples of emancipatory labor in the forms of collective knowledge production and collective bookmaking. Both projects are informed by the democratic, non-sexist, non-homophobic, horizontal leadership approach to liberatory labor that ankhing seeks to privilege.

Chapter 4 explores this present historical moment's virulent anti-Blackness in the United States, and how, as Erica R. Edwards suggests, fiction can be a resource for forging political contestation through "the formal achievement of *curiosity*: a politics and aesthetics of serious interrogation, playful questioning, thoughtful, puzzling, and fantastic reinvention." Historically, the Black subject has been the testing ground for State-sponsored oppression aimed at America's most marginalized subjects, so a specific exploration of thoughtful, inventive, and politically-engaged Black literatures will be generative in understanding American-style oppression and resistance. By reading the superbly-curious, fantastically-imaginative, and Spirit-infused work of Kamau Daáood and Wanda Coleman, this final chapter argues that very creative and inventive cultural production can serve as a technology to expand Black subjectivity, and serve as a counterforce to sovereign and societal pressures that move Black subjects toward bare life.

1

A Matter of Body and Soul in *The People of Paper* and *Mumbo Jumbo*

> And if we had learned anything from this story it was to be cautious of paper—to be mindful of its fragile construction and sharp edges, but mostly to be cautious of what is written on it.[1]
>
> —Salvador Plascencia

> Well, Moses went on stage and began gyrating his hips and singing the words of the Book of Thoth, and a strange thing happened. The ears of the people began to bleed.[2]
>
> —Ishmael Reed

Paper Cuts

The Introduction argues that the State has aggressively pushed African-American and Latinx subjects down the human animacy scale (a scale notating qualities of agency, awareness, mobility, and aliveness) toward bare life, via sociopolitical and juridical means. As an indigenous spiritual iteration of animacy, the Egyptian ankh powers the liberatory ankhing process, whereby groups organize themselves to resist hegemonic forces that seek to delimit their subjectivity and agency—and their ability to be fully alive. Ultimately, the Introduction argues that American literatures is a repository to reimagine new possibilities for African American, Latinx, and other disenfranchised communities to resist bare life and elevate their animacy. Through reading avant-garde Black and Brown literatures, chapter 1 argues that ankhing's valorization of community folkways, Spirit, and art contribute to the elevation of Latinx and African-American animacy.

Books can paper cut. Ishmael Reed's *Mumbo Jumbo* and Salvador Plascencia's *The People of Paper* represent the lacerating potential of narrative on paper. The novels function as commentaries on knowledge production, the relationship between knowledge and power, and how written knowledge cuts racialized subjects in two: bare life ("wounded, expendable, and endangered") and good life ("life tethered to political agency and speech").

The *Oxford English Dictionary* notes that the origin of "cut" is unknown, but the *OED* suggests that the word's earliest appearance (including "cutt" and "cutte") occurs before 1300 CE; its denotation bears no apparent connection to cut's more familiar sixteenth-century Modern English signification, "The act or result of cutting."[3] The pre-1300 entry reads: "1. =Lot: in the phrase draw cuts (or *lay* cut) applied to a ready way of casting lots, by the chance of drawing sticks or straws of unequal lengths . . . he who chances to draw the bit differing in length is the person to whom the lot falls."[4] The earliest appearance of cut dealt with difference—and its consequences. In *Mumbo Jumbo* and *The People of Paper*, subjects come up short when they draw cuts defined by their racialized bodies. The unequal ways in which colored bodies are marked result in unequal treatment for colored bodies. Yet, there is a dialectical aspect to the cut, to difference. Difference informs and defines "standard," as oppressed informs and defines oppressor. There is liberatory power in difference, liberatory power in the cut. The cut's power is apparent in the improvisational act (and vernacular phrase) of turning a lemon into lemonade. Fred Moten offers a cutting derivation on this theme:

> What is needed is an improvisation of the transition from descent to cut, an audition of the ancient prefiguring trace of the cut in the depths, an activation of lingering by and in the cut (and of the possibility of action and lingering and the promise of freedom in action).[5]

The ankh is an ancient liberatory technology rooted in indigenous spirituality. The ankh's indigeneity signifies its difference from State-sanctioned American Christianity and signifies its promise of freedom in action. The ankh challenges the State's hegemonic sovereignty by *existing* as an oppositional spiritual power source to the Christian Sovereign that the State sanctions—the Sovereign that, during slavery and afterwards, sanctioned the State's efforts to push racialized subjects in the direction of bare life.

Flower Pickers and Revolution

In *The People of Paper*, El Monte (a primarily Latinx city 13 miles east of downtown Los Angeles) residents begin to engage a Sovereign-like force intruding on their lives. Saturn—the sovereign, and a near homophone for the word "sovereign"—seems to have a sophisticated spying apparatus. Saturn tracks the Latinx residents' comings, goings, public meetings, and, at times, has access to their private conversations. The El Monte sovereign's surveillance power "is of a piercing strength able to penetrate asbestos and wood shingles, tar paper, plywood, the darkness of the attic."[6] This intense sovereign encroachment is coupled with agricultural laborers' harsh sociopolitical and economic realities, including a "plantation [that] paid thirty cents for each pound of carnations and fifty for the thorny stems of roses."[7] In a neoliberal context, the aforementioned labor realities help to produce:

> the first street gang born of carnations. But for them there was no softness in petals and no aroma in flowers. They felt only splinters and calluses from tilling the land and smelled only the stench of fertilizer and horse shit. Their shoes were wet and the cuffs of their work pants crusted with mud. At midday they took off their shirts wringing the sweat and then tossing them over their shoulders. And always a cutting knife was in hand.[8]

Tired of their lives moving toward bare life, El Monte community members decide to organize themselves and fight back. An agricultural worker in the floral industry-dominated city, Federico de la Fe aligns with the local gang EMF (El Monte Flores) and begins to organize resistance efforts against the sovereign. Froggy, a veteran EMF gang member, recounts an early Federico de la Fe recruitment meeting directed at EMF gangsters. "[Federico de la Fe] said it was a war for volition and against the commodification of sadness. 'It is a war against the fate that has been decided for us.'"⁹

Federico de la Fe speaks of a war against fate. A war against fate suggests an unwinnable war against what has already been determined; it signifies a battle against the lot, the cut one has drawn in life. However, the cut thrust upon the El Monte flower pickers, these citizens with knives at-the-ready, is not a cut of their own choosing. The cut at hand is a hand-me-down cut from a sovereign on high. During the recruitment meeting, Froggy "asked who had given us this fate. Federico de la Fe shook his head and said that he was not entirely sure. All he could tell was that it was something or someone in the sky."¹⁰ This gap between the citizen's cut, and how the cut came to be, is where enough hope resides to engage in an unwinnable war. If a citizen doesn't choose the cut, maybe the citizen's fate is not sealed: volition can have its say.

The exercise of human agency amidst extraordinary obstacles, the making of a way out of no way, bespeaks to the experiences of many racialized subjects in the United States: captured Africans surviving the Atlantic Ocean Middle Passage to endure the Mississippi River Middle Passage and prodigal Mexicans surviving passage along the Rio Grande to their ancestral homelands, where their native bodies are now marked as alien in former Mexican territory. In the context of expansive discrimination, degradation, and death-dealing, what is the relationship between volition, desire, and resistance? Fred Moten avers, "To act on the desire to be the opposite, the desire not to collaborate, is to object. How might resistance suspend the process of subjection?"¹¹

Federico de la Fe, the flower picker, decides not to collaborate with the sovereign power who has drawn a lot, a cut, for him to live out: bare life. Despite the overwhelming odds, he is compelled by volition to fight an unwinnable war against fate by choosing the opposite of bare life. Federico de la Fe desires and picks the "good life"—a life tethered to political agency and speech. Federico de la Fe exercises his political agency by calling a meeting of local gang members and speaking resistance to them. "[If] we fight we might be able to gain control, to shield ourselves and live our lives for ourselves."¹² Federico de la Fe is making an affective appeal to EMF. The community activist wants to *move* them to believe that the good life is possible for "[T]he first street gang born of carnations," who feel "only splinters and calluses from tilling the land and smelled only the stench of fertilizer and horse shit."

As a resistance organizer, Federico de la Fe is operating as an actant, "a source of action that can be either human or nonhuman . . . which has efficacy, can do things, has sufficient coherence to make a difference, produce effects, alter the course of events." Employing speech-tethered affect, Federico de la Fe is seeking to alter the course of events through a resistance movement by, as Chen writes, affectively engaging "many bodies at once." The resistance leader is attempting to move racialized bodies, Brown matter, away from bare life toward the good life. Federico de la Fe animates this process by discouraging gangster flower pickers from collaborating with a sovereign force determined to draw unsavory cuts on their behalf.

Along with defining the battle as a war against fate, Federico de la Fe defines the battle as a war against the "commodification of sadness." The bare life is a sad life. Removed from political agency and speech (and under the atomizing gaze of a sovereign), an El Monte Latinx agricultural worker's bare life slides down the human animacy scale toward animality: a kind of subhuman object. The flower picker's bare life becomes "sadness itself," the "sad thing itself"; thingified, the El Monte agricultural worker becomes a candidate for commodification. In "Estranged Labor," Marx writes that the worker:

> does not feel content but unhappy, does not develop freely his physical and mental energy . . . the worker's activity is not his spontaneous activity. It belongs to another; it is the loss of his self. As a result, therefore, man (the worker) no longer feels himself to be freely active in any but his animal functions—eating, drinking, procreating, and in his human functions he no longer feels himself to be anything but an animal. What is animal becomes human and what is human becomes animal.[13]

Marx writes above about the worker whose fate is determined by a capitalist system (a socioeconomic representative of the sovereign) determined to exploit the worker's surplus labor. Marx's solution is to foment a revolutionary resistance movement to overturn the sovereign's system. Federico de la Fe has a similar strategy. The initial recruitment and organizing meeting with EMF's disenfranchised members is representative of the ankhing process's initial element: individuals and groups organizing themselves to resist hegemonic forces, which seek to delimit their subjectivity, social, political, and economic agency, and delimit their power to determine their own life courses. Federico de la Fe's war of volition against the commodification of sadness signifies that collective will is necessary to determine community life courses—and collective will is necessary to resist becoming a community of commodities.

Liberated Woman

Subcomandante Sandra's role in *The People of Paper* highlights another element of the ankhing process. As the Introduction addresses, male-led liberation movements in the twentieth century have been taken to task for trying to circumscribe and undermine women's roles in emancipatory labor. Harris argues that women have been pushed toward "support roles" that don't fully respect their potential leadership, organizing efficacy, and strategic contributions to the cause at hand. Misogyny in liberation movements is harmful to female (and male) emancipatory laborers' morale, motivation, and effectiveness—and misogyny is a costly strategic move.

Constricting women's contributions to freedom work constricts liberatory resources from movements that traditionally are "out-resourced" by the hegemonic power structures they are resisting. Strategically, it is wise to encourage full participation from all willing liberatory laborers, especially those whose gendered subject positions may result in a more comprehensive best practices pool. As a literary theory technology, with pragmatic, real-world liberatory applications, ankhing champions an inclusive approach to liberatory labor.

Subcomandante Sandra's emancipatory role in *The People of Paper* is a productive arena to explore inclusive approaches to liberatory labor which ankhing encourages. Ankhing's second element is defined as a process in sociopolitical and economic struggle, whereby inspiration, strategy and communal labor comingle to serve subjugated subjects in their efforts to collectively think through the most effective means to resist hegemonic forces—and through this idea-exchange, inspire, motivate, and move each other toward best practices to resist hegemonic forces, seeking to delimit their subjectivity, social, political, and economic agency, and delimit their power to determine their own life courses. This process includes rigorous self-interrogation and group interrogation toward creating a healthy, whole, ankhing process that can result in healthy, whole, ankhing best practices and outcomes.

In the El Monte Flores revolutionary campaign against the sovereign hegemon Saturn, Sandra is promoted to subcomandante and is selected for a critical leadership position. As Subcomandante Sandra, she has jurisdiction over new EMF member initiations. Only EMF gang members are trusted enough to engage in the revolutionary struggle against Saturn. Federico de la Fe's exclusive utilization of gang members, and their humanizing depiction in the novel, serves as a powerful counternarrative to gang members' routine demonization. As the revolutionary in charge of initiating new gang members in a liberation struggle, Subcomandante Sandra has the power to vet each potential emancipatory worker. Philosophically, Federico de la Fe embraces the untapped liberatory potential of one of America's most demonized populations; Subcomandante Sandra's charge is to transform these gangsters' liberatory potential into liberatory effectiveness. As a female leader in a primarily male organization, Subcomandante Sandra brings an alternative subject position and concomitant approach to leadership—and through her success, highlights the emancipatory benefits of inclusivity and intra-group difference.

As a member of El Monte's racialized community, which has drawn the cut of underclass and political disenfranchisement, Subcomandante Sandra draws the cut of gender difference and employs its leadership benefits toward her community's efforts to resist being "[s]tripped from political significance and exposed to murderous violence." In order for a potential new member to join El Monte Flores, they have to show their courage and fighting skills by going through a "brinca." A brinca is the "being jumped into the gang" process, whereby the potential recruit has to simultaneously fight six current EMF members. The novel implies that before Subcomandante Sandra's rise in leadership, the six members selected for the brinca were the most violent EMF gangsters; this strategy was employed to test the new gang member's toughness. Subcomandante Sandra approaches the brinca differently:

> [Subcomandante] Sandra coordinated the initiations; though she honored the traditions of EMF, she did so in the kindest way, electing the meekest members for the brincas, sparing as [sic] much injuries as possible.[14]

The passage above, narrated by the former brinca organizer, Froggy, suggests that Subcomandante Sandra did not think the "testing toughness" approach to initiating new EMF members was the best practice. The above passage indicates that the "testing toughness" approach was creating excessive injuries, which were counterproductive to resisting the hegemonic forces delimiting EMF life courses and pushing them toward bare life.

However, it is important to note that after the implied group interrogation of the former initiation practice (which Subcomandante Sandra determined not to be the best practice), she doesn't completely eliminate the brinca practice. Instead, the new initiation leader Subcomandante Sandra "honored the traditions of EMF," via maintaining the practice, but adjusted its implementation by "electing the meekest members for the brincas, sparing as much injuries as possible." Subcomandante Sandra's nuanced method of best practice creation and implementation indicates a collectivist leadership style that considers results and process. Completely discarding the inherently violent brinca practice would have resulted in a reduction of even more injuries but could have fomented dissent among members who value EMF traditions. Subcomandante Sandra balances best practices for the liberation movement with best practices that will be accepted by liberation movement members. This balancing act indicates a leadership capacity not previously exhibited by second in command EMF member Comandante Froggy, the previous initiation director—who promoted Subcomandante Sandra into her position.

Before her promotion, Subcomandante Sandra had been romantically involved with Comandante Froggy, but after her promotion, she initiated changes in the relationship. Comandante Froggy describes the change by saying, "She discussed only battle strategy and logistics in my presence and refused to acknowledge anything I said unless I called her "Subcomandante Sandra."[15]

It is not difficult to imagine people engaged in liberation struggle becoming romantically involved, especially if they are in close proximity. Essentially, Comandante Froggy promotes his girlfriend. However, it is noteworthy that Subcomandante Sandra is committed to establishing respect through her effective emancipatory labor leadership in the public realm (i.e., developing more effective initiation best practices) but also in her private domain relationship with boyfriend/Comandante Froggy. By maintaining liberatory labor-oriented conversations and insisting on the use of her liberatory labor title, Subcomandante Sandra changes the dynamic within her private relationship. As the new initiation leader is struggling for community emancipation, she is struggling for private emancipation as well. Subcomandante Sandra's private emancipation struggle is a fictionalized and real-world referent to the often invisible struggles liberatory women confront within their homes' private domains: the struggle for physical safety, the struggle for respect, and the struggle to determine their own life courses.

The novel further illuminates this private struggle when it reveals that Subcomandante Sandra's father had been so physically abusive throughout her childhood that she eventually moved into Froggy's home. When Subcomandante Sandra's father comes to retrieve her from Froggy's home, Froggy cuts her father's throat with a carnation knife. Subcomandante Sandra's response gives insight into the intersection of gendered, private emancipatory struggle and gendered, community emancipatory struggle:

> [E]ven though my whole life I wanted to flee from my father I did not like seeing him wrapped in the shreds of my shawl and buried in the middle of a flower field. I remained subcomandante of EMF but moved out of Froggy's. I could not sleep in the same room with the man who had killed my father. [I] moved into a stucco at the edge of El Monte. I slept alone, cushioned by rugs and pillows. I was a quiet sleeper and did not thrash about or even snore, but I began to wake with welts on my arms and my ribs sore and bruised. It was not until I looked in the mirror and noticed the black eye on my face that I knew I had been dreaming of my father.[16]

Throughout the narrative, the novel suggests that Subcomandante Sandra grew up in an El Monte agricultural labor family—the type of family she was helping to create best practices for to fight a sovereign committed to delimiting El Monte agricultural laborers' life courses and pushing them toward bare life. Her "whole life" Subcomandante Sandra wanted "to flee" and liberate herself from a father she was likely trying to liberate, despite the fact that he "beat her so much that she could no longer remember what it was like to properly knit."[17]

Subcomandante Sandra's ironic and oppressive private context makes her public emancipatory effectiveness more impressive and instructive. The effectiveness is impressive, because Subcomandante Sandra has to first self-liberate in order to engage in community liberation; her effectiveness is instructive, because negotiating private-arena, gendered oppression equips her with an enhanced skillset that translates into negotiating public arena community oppression—a specific enhancement that a male EMF leader is unlikely to possess given the specifically gendered way the skillset is developed. Subcomandante Sandra's experience operates as an argument for gender diversity and inclusivity within liberation movement leadership; her experience is also why ankhing promotes gender diversity and inclusivity for its strategic and equitable benefits.

Subcomandante Sandra's EMF leadership role is a constructive space to examine another aspect of ankhing's focus on creating a healthy, whole, ankhing process that can result in healthy, whole, ankhing practices and outcomes. "Whole" is pivotal here. Considering a liberation laborer's whole life (as opposed to just the parts that specifically relate to emancipatory thought and action) is essential to creating effective activism. When emancipatory leadership considers an emancipatory worker's whole life, it can promote community activism that considers community members' whole lives, which is to say, their material conditions, their children and aged parents, and their emotional, psychological, and physical health. When a whole life is considered, it signifies that both liberatory workers and community members are whole human beings with expansive subjectivities, and not just activists with a job to do, or oppressed folk who need to be organized and liberated.

Federico de la Fe is a single father raising his pre-teen daughter Little Merced. As a result, Federico de la Fe's resistance leader and father roles are coterminous. When Merced menstruates for the first time, the novel highlights the practical ways in which an activist's personal and political lives can overlap:

> "I ran out of my room into the kitchen, yelling for my father. He saw the blood and stood up, but not before covering his notes with a jagged slab of lead."
> "It's Saturn," I said.

He laughed and then wrung a wet towel over the kitchen sink and then handed it to me.

He said not to worry, that everything would be okay, and then picked up the phone.

"Subcomandante Sandra."[18]

It is significant that the resistance leader's daughter thinks her menstrual bleeding is being caused by the sovereign force Saturn. Liberation workers with children are liberation workers who are exposing their children to the powerful forces seeking to delimit their life courses. At times, the exposure to such forces have unexpected consequences, like children attributing intimate body functions to an external hegemon.

Should activism begin at home? Should activists teach their preteen children emancipatory work, if they know that exposure to the work may inflict psychological and/or physical damage? What is the cost of not teaching activism at home? These are the questions that liberation workers with children must confront, along with dilemmas relating to childcare, school transportation, and menstruation. The effective handling of these private concerns is what allows activists to engage in public activist work, including door-knocking, information distribution, fundraising, and community meetings.

When Federico de la Fe's daughter Little Merced begins to menstruate for the first time, he calls one of the leaders in his resistance movement for assistance. Most likely, Federico de la Fe calls Subcomandante Sandra, because there is often a trust factor that comes with shared leadership. Also, one could argue that Federico de la Fe uses Little Merced's first menstruation as an opportunity to intimately introduce his daughter to a potential liberatory role model. Subcomandante Sandra humanizes liberation labor by addressing a shared gendered need:

> I showed Little Merced how to use the napkin and mix a vinegar wash. Because we lived within the ashen boundaries, Little Merced would start her cycle at the same time I and every other woman in El Monte did. In El Monte, sisterhood and solidarity were always marked by bloodshed. I pummeled girls on the mouth [during EMF initiations], their blood spilling out of their chins and onto

my knuckles. And then I nursed their broken skin, put arnica compounds on their bruises, and welcomed them into EMF. I hiked up my dress and pulled my underwear down, exposing the stained quilted pad. 'See, I'm just like you,' I said. Little Merced nodded. I hugged her and left Federico de la Fe's house.[19]

Subcomandante Sandra addresses Little Merced's specific private need by showing her "how to use the napkin and mix a vinegar wash"; simultaneously, the resistance leader frames the interaction as an ushering of the pre-teen subject into El Monte "sisterhood." It is a sisterhood and solidarity "marked by bloodshed." Little Merced joins a women's circle with coordinated bloodshed from uterine walls and ritualized bloodshed "spilling out of their chins." Combined, both kinds of bloodshed signify a female subject who has matured enough to engage in battle against a sovereign determined to delimit her life course—and the life courses of those who share her bloodline and community.

Similar to Federico de la Fe, Subcomandante Sandra is operating as an actant: "a source of action that can be either human or nonhuman . . . has efficacy, can do things, has sufficient coherence to make a difference, produce effects, alter the course of events." As a leader among a community of women—and a leader of men—Subcomandante Sandra is able to articulate the power of community by saying to a young female community member, "See, I'm just like you." Female resistance leader Subcomandante Sandra is also declaring, by extension, to Little Merced, "See, you are just like me." Subcomandante Sandra's declaration is a subtle and powerful move; through her own personal vulnerability, Subcomandante Sandra is accessing the vulnerable, private space of a young female community member to help lay the foundation for Little Merced's entrance into the public space of emancipatory labor. Subcomandante Sandra's strategic move aligns with ankhing's dictum that a "whole" (private and public) approach is the most effective means to resist hegemonic forces; strategically, this whole approach can eventually inspire, motivate, and move Little Merced toward taking the liberatory actions to implement the specific best practices to resist hegemonic forces that are trying to push the women, men, and youth in her community toward bare life.

The Life and Times of Jes Grew

Ishmael Reed's *Mumbo Jumbo* is a novel concerned with life and living—and the forces determined to delimit life and living. Similar to *The People of Paper*'s Latinx subjects, *Mumbo Jumbo*'s narrative features fictionalized African-American subjects resisting an aggressive push towards bare life. In *Mumbo Jumbo*, subjects are not only resisting being "[s]tripped from political significance and exposed to murderous violence," they are resisting being stripped from their very souls—and soul itself.

As this project's Introduction lays out, in *Spirituals and the Blues*, Cone argues that soulful Black artists are expressing an indwelling God-energy, an indwelling spiritual energy, which manifests as an iteration of "life" that can enhance emancipatory labor. The soul of Black folk can liberate Black folk. Black artists can animate life in disenfranchised communities enough to enhance community members' ability to resist being pushed toward bare life, and struggle toward what Agamben calls the "good life"—life tethered to "political agency and speech."

In *Mumbo Jumbo*, there is a version of this art-tethered, Black soul energy that can move subjects away from bare life and toward the good life; it is called Jes Grew. "Jes Grew has no end and no beginning . . . We will miss it for awhile but it will come back, and when it returns we will see that it never left. You see, life will never end; there is really no end to life, if anything goes it will be death. Jes Grew is life."[20] In *Mumbo Jumbo*'s narrative, the Atonists, a powerful collection of anti-Blackness hegemons, including Masons, Knights Templar, and Teutonic Knights are dedicated to suppressing and ultimately destroying the Black soul expression Jes Grew. Strategically, if the Atonists can destroy Jes Grew, destroy Black Spirit, destroy Black soul, there will be no force powerful enough to counteract the hegemonic force moving Black subjects toward bare life. A complementary concern for the Atonists is that Black soul is "spreading" to some White subjects, creating a potentially powerful ally class for the Black community. In *The People of Paper*, a historically and socioeconomically marginalized subpopulation (Latinx gang members) serve as a Latinx community's resistance fighters; in *Mumbo Jumbo*, a historically and socioeconomically marginalized subpopulation (Black artists) serve as

Jes Grew's—and a Black community's—resistance brigade. The narrative explains that anti-Black forces "will try to depress Jes Grew but it will only spring back and prosper. We will make our own future Text. A future generation of young artists will accomplish this."[21] The attempt to "depress Jes Grew" is a hegemonic attempt to depress Jes Grew's functionality as an actant, depress its "sufficient coherence to make a difference, produce effects, alter the course of events."

Jes Grew, this corollary to the Black Spirit, offers an opportunity to think critically about the power available to some soulful Black artists to help initiate change and alter the course of events—without "romanticizing" the artist in the process. This study argues that some soulful Black artists have the power to inspire and move disenfranchised subjects toward liberatory thought and action and away from bare life. Black artists' relatively marginalized and alienated subject positions in their own communities, ironically, positions them as potential freedom fighters for their communities. Moten acknowledges the latent power of the alienated when he writes, "[A]lienation and distance represent the critical possibility of freedom."[22] *Mumbu Jumbo* suggests that Black soulful artists, operating as a liberatory vanguard, will create a Black community's "own future Text." Contextualized by Moten's alienation move, this statement can be read as soulful Black artists "write the future Story" of a Black community by creating liberatory art informed by their own alienation. Identifying soulful Blacks artists as an alienated subpopulation who can alter the course of events, is not romanticizing artists, it is identifying soulful Black artists as a subpopulation who can employ the "Spirit," the Jes Grew, to powerfully enhance their own animacy in order to affect and animate their community toward liberatory thought and action.

To further distance soulful Black artists' emancipatory power from the romantic artist notion, it may be helpful to explore how power is produced by Spirit's internal workings and architecture. In the Spirit qua emancipatory power context, Latour would be interested in what the Spirit can "do," or, in the Black vernacular, "how it do, what it do." Improvisation is often one element present when the Spirit do what it do. Addressing actants, Latour writes, "I never act; I am always slightly surprised by what I do . . . That which acts through me is also surprised by what I do, by the chance to mutate, to change."[23] Improvisation is the art and the power of surprise; improvisation is the undetermined, or indeterminacy, made manifest in music, or

Spirit, or literatures. Henry Louis Gates, Jr. frames *Mumbo Jumbo* as a text about indeterminacy. "It is indeterminacy, the sheer plurality of meaning, the very play of the signifier itself, which *Mumbo Jumbo* celebrates . . . Its central character Jes Grew, cannot be reduced by the Atonists, as they complain: 'It's nothing we can bring into focus or categorize; once we call it 1 thing it forms into something else.'"[24]

In the jazz improvisational moment, the indeterminacy moment, the trust that the right series of notes to play will reveal themselves at the appropriate moment requires a certain level of belief, faith. The indeterminacy moment requires a faith that the Spirit will provide a salvific intercession, so that the unplanned music will not falter. Indeterminacy requires the courage to embrace the reality that the music *will* falter at times—and embrace the reality that the failure will happen in front of an audience.

This risk of failure is one of the reasons why jazz improvisation is exciting for some musicians. It is a courting of danger. For some audiences, improvisation is often exciting for a similar reason. Improvisation is an opportunity to witness someone taking real risks in a public forum. Public improvisation titillates similar to the way that people gather to watch a human being walk across a high wire between two buildings: public failure is a real—and exciting—possibility. When public faltering is realized it becomes a public spectacle. Public failure as spectacle is a grotesque type of entertainment. Therefore, even the *possibility* of public failure is entertaining. The artist producing art in this high-risk context is articulating and embodying a type of freedom; it is a liberatory modality that melds the creative and the sociopolitical. This high-risk improvisational art functions as the artist's interlocutor with her community: "I am free from form and expectations; I am free-form and create anticipation." Poet Kamau Daáood's ode to prodigious improviser and saxophonist John Coltrane, "Liberator of the Spirit," speaks of freedom and form: "John Coltrane was a freedom fighter/liberator of the Spirit from the shackles of form/expanding beyond the boundaries/blow away decay."[25]

Given the traditionally disenfranchised subject position of Black artists, one can read the John Coltrane referent "John Coltrane was a freedom fighter/liberator of the Spirit from the shackles of form" as a sociopolitical signifier. Black artists as resistance fighters are resisting objectification and resisting the push into the form known as bare life. In order for this resistance to be possible, the Spirit must be liberated "from the shackles of form," because the Spirit is the liberatory power source. A liberated Spirit makes possible a more expansive subjectivity. When there is more expansive subjectivity, it is possible for the Black subject to "expand beyond the boundaries," boundaries which are being defined by actants positioned higher on the animacy hierarchy. A liberated Spirit and more expansive subjectivity allows Black subjects to resist being hailed and defined as *homo sacer*.

Black Spirit and the Freedom Boogie

This project acknowledges the problematics involved in theorizing about Spirit concepts like Jes Grew. How does one critically engage the esoteric without floating in the badlands of unverifiable, rootless conjecture? This problem is further complicated when race is introduced in the form of Black Spirit, because it increases the danger of the aforementioned badlands expanding into unverifiable, *essentialist*, rootless conjecture. Jane Bennett's exploration of critical vitalism may provide a fire trail through this problematic terrain.

Critical vitalism was an early twentieth-century philosophoscientific movement that congealed around the work of Henri Bergson and Hans Driesch. Kantian-inspired, both thinkers wrestled with the "What is life" question by interrogating the nature of the "vital force" that animated matter.[26] Following Kant, both theorists were careful to separate this vital force from a spiritual imperative; they "distinguished themselves from those 'naïve' vitalists who posited a spiritual force or soul that was immune to any scientific or experimental inquiry."[27] In the critical vitalism context, Bergson's élan vital notion will be most productive for this discussion:

> Bergson's [élan vital] is also based on the distinction between Life and matter . . . Life names a certain *propensity* for 'the utmost possible' activeness, a bias in favor of mobile and morphing states. Likewise, matter must be understood as *leaning* toward passivity, a tendency in favor of stable formations . . . [L]ife is not susceptible to quantification . . . Life 'splays' itself out in new forms that are not even conceivable before they exist, says Bergson, and were they to be quantified and measured, it would already be too late, for life will have moved on.[28]

Like Jes Grew, Bergson's free-moving, animating life force, élan vital, is defined by a "propensity for 'the utmost possible' activeness, a bias in favor of mobile and morphing states." Élan vital is the infinite possibility of agency, movement, and change. Élan vital is liberated. The indeterminate nature and infinite number of expressive options—the infinite freedom of expression—makes élan vital unquantifiable; these qualities make it that which cannot be fully known. However, élan vital can be seen and felt because of the effects and affect it produces. This understanding of élan vital is reminiscent of Cone's understanding of the Black Spirit from the Introduction:

> [The Black Spiritual] is a faithful free response to the movement of the Black Spirit. It is the movement of the Black Spirit. It is the Black Spirit. It is the Black community accepting themselves as the people of the Black Spirit and knowing through the chains of his presence that no chains can hold the Spirit of Black humanity in bondage.[29]

Both Black Spirit and élan vital privilege movement. The Black Spirit is tethered to "free response" and the élan vital is connected to "infinite freedom of expression." Both notions are deeply concerned with the relationship between liberation and "life." However, unlike Black Spirit, and its fictional counterpart Jes Grew, élan vital's philosopho-scientific underpinnings are distinguished from "religious notions of the soul; [Bergson] also rejected the idea that the vital force could have any existence apart from the bodies in which it operated."[30] Departing from Bergson and Bennett, this study argues that the vital force can have existence outside the body in which it operates—and can be spread from person to person—like the Jes Grew virus. In *Spirituals & the Blues*, Cone describes the scene in the Macedonia A.M.E. church where the Spirit is "breaking into the lives of the people." Cone alludes to the well-known traditional Black church practice of a member "catching the Holy Spirit" and that Spirit breaking into person after person as it spreads throughout the congregation.

Like the "Holy Dance" that is often symptomatic of a church member who has caught the Holy Spirit, "dance mania" is a symptom of Jes Grew and a symbol of freedom:

> Dance manias inundate the land. J. A. Rogers, writes, 'It is just the epidemic contagiousness of jazz that makes it, like

> measles, sweep the block.' People do the Charleston, the Texas Tommy, and other anonymously created symptoms of Jes Grew. The Wallflower Order remembers the 10th Century *tarantism* which nearly threatened the survival of the Church. Even Paracelus, a 'radical' who startled the academicians by lecturing in the vernacular, terms these manias a 'disease.'[31]

In order for the Spirit to travel from person to person like a liberatory airborne virus, like a deliverance disease, it has to be able to exist "outside the body in which it operates" during the journey from person to person. This Spirit that can travel through a congregation is the same Spirit that can travel through The World Stage Performance Gallery jazz audience when the soul-stirring jazz singer Dwight Trible is frenzying through "Mothership"; it is the same Spirit that can move through The World Stage Writer's Workshop when poet Kamau Daáood is trancing through "Papa Lean Griot"; it is the same Spirit that can move through The Essence Music Festival audience when soulful crooner Jill Scott is hitting low-down, high-notes on "One"; it is the same Spirit that can make hundreds of heads bounce in unison at The Forum as hip hop artist Kendrick Lamar chants through "Alright" then explodes into "Humble." Soulful artists can be conduits for the Spirit.

When soulful artists are also engaged in social justice work, the Spirit moving through them is an actant in social justice movements;[32] the Spirit operating in them, and as them, performs the critical work of fomenting group action. Socially engaged artists can facilitate the process whereby community members are moved significantly enough to "catch the Spirit" of heightened social justice commitment by witnessing community members around them being moved significantly enough to "catch the Spirit" of heightened social justice commitment.[33] This initial Spirit-catching process is not sufficient to maintain commitment, but it functions as an affective foundation on which to build a sustainable future commitment to social justice. At times, socially engaged artists are positioned as inspiring "opening acts" or "conscious entertainment" in between emancipatory speakers on social justice programs, rallies, and direct actions. However, this study argues the Spirit that can make soulful, socially engaged artists inspiring as "creative filler" is the same Spirit that can make them effective leaders in social justice movements. In the emancipatory labor context, this project seeks to move artists from margin to center.

Liberatory Art Thieves

In *Mumbo Jumbo*, there is a liberatory organization that centers artists as leaders, strategists, and intelligence agents. *Mu'tafikah* is an international force of specialized agents who liberate art and cultural artifacts produced by people of color but controlled by European and American interests. *Mu'tafikah*'s efforts are ancillary to Jes Grew—and vice versa—because both are concerned with liberation. Jes Grew "is compounded by the *Mu'tafikah* who are responsible for art thefts now ravishing private collections of Europe and America. 1 of their number, an international *Mu'tafikah*, has lifted the sacred Papyri of Ani stored in the British Museum and returned it to 'Brothers in Cairo.'"[34] The *Mu'tafikah* members' subject positions as artists of color contribute to their very specialized art-centric mission. The fact that artists lead the organization likely plays a role in the strategic determination that art repatriation is a revolutionary act worth risking *Mu'tafifkah* members' liberty and possibly their lives. In *Mumbo Jumbo*, artists who are leaders value art's liberatory power.

Mu'tafikah's international, multiracial profile also speaks to their desire to support "Third World" liberation struggles. In their underground headquarters:

> *Mu'tafikah* are carefully packing items. They are to be sent to a contact 'Frank' somewhere in the Pacific Islands who will in turn ship them to their rightful owners in Asia. 'Tam' a Nigerian musician and writer will return 5000 masks and wood sculptures to Africa. He had begun by lifting a Benin bronze plaque with leopard from the Linden-Museum in Stuttgart, Germany . . . [Tam] repatriated masks and figures—carried to Europe as booty from Nigeria Gold Coast, Upper Volta and the Ivory Coast . . . Another [agent], a South African trumpeter, 'Hugh,' is in L.A. transmitting Black American sounds on home. He realizes

that the essential Pan-Africanism is artists relating across continents their craft, drumbeats from the aeons, sounds that are still with us.[35]

The nomenclature "repatriated" is significant. In the 1950s and 1960s, there was a well-known wave of African students who studied at European and American universities and repatriated back to their home countries. Many repatriated African students employed their broadened skillsets in homeland liberation struggles.[36] "[Tam] repatriated masks and figures" suggests more than a simple return of "booty" that had been "carried to Europe." Given the Third World Liberation context, repatriated signifies a liberation-aligned significance for the masks and figures.

The West's systematic pillaging of African resources (including African peoples), during and after the Atlantic Slave Trade, depressed African subjects' relative animacy, decimated local and national economies, and devalued African cultural production. The fact that *Mu'tafikah* countrymen and allies are willing to risk liberty and life to repatriate art enhances the perceived value of African cultural production. The art repatriation suggests that art is "worth" death and that art is as "valuable" as life, which is to say, defying death and living life for African art enhances African art's value—while enhancing African diasporic animacy.[37]

Through South African *Mu'tafikah* "Hugh's" cultural labor, Reed argues that "essential Pan-Africanism is artists relating across continents their craft." Reed reframes Pan-Africanism (a political philosophy that supports African diasporic political and economic unity) as a political philosophy promoting artistic cultural exchange that centers art. The relatively privileged positioning of Western art vis-à-vis non-Western art speaks to the relatively privileged positioning of Western subjects vis-à-vis non-Western subjects. Generally, the dialectics between cultural product and cultural producer allows a relatively higher valuation for Western art, because Western subjects are its creators. In a neoliberal context where bodies and life itself are commodities whose perceived values are racially influenced, the relatively higher animacy of Western subjects is undergirded by their alignment with art that is more highly valued. By extension, enhancing the relative value of non-Western art, African art in particular, is a political technology that enhances the value and animacy of African subjects. When

African subjects possess more animacy, more life, it is more difficult to demonize African life. With less demonization, it is easier to resist the push into bare life. In this context, *Mu'tafikah*'s risking of liberty and life to repatriate African art becomes a revolutionary enterprise. Reed suggests that repatriating Black art potentially revolutionizes how the African Diaspora views itself. Furthermore, Reed suggests that repatriating Black art has the potential to revolutionize how the West (through the prism of African subject-created art) views African subjects.

The *Mu'tafikah* headquarters operates as a counterpublic: an artistic heterotopia of resistance. From the Introduction, Frasier avers that counterpublics help "subordinated peoples formulate oppositional interpretations of their identities, interests and needs." *Mu'tafikah*'s oppositional interpretation is a political philosophy interpretation that privileges art as a revolutionary technology. Kohn argues that heterotopias of resistance are "sites for political emancipation; their function is social transformation . . . [Heterotopias of resistance] are sites that foster oppositional practices by sheltering counterhegemonic ideas and identities." In a three-story building's basement on Chinatown's edge, the *Mu'tafikah* headquarters is a site where alternative ideas about art's emancipatory role drive the group's social transformation goal. This art-based, liberatory approach is not meant to replace historically oppressed people's traditional forms of socioeconomic and political resistance work; the approach is designed to serve as a complement to traditional resistance work.

As the Introduction argues about artistic heterotopias of resistance, artistic can refer to a previously "non-artistic site" that has been transformed into an artistic site. A basement in a three-story building on Chinatown's edge has been repurposed as an art redistribution center. *Mu'tafikah* headquarters is not a site where international art is visited by the Westerners but a Western weigh station where prodigal art stops on its way back to its country of origin. *Mu'tafikah* headquarters is the anti-museum: art comes to the people, as opposed to the people coming to the art.

The *Mu'tafikah* anti-museum construct is both an explicit and implicit attack on traditional Western museums. The construct's explicit element is defined by the physical attack, the breeching of the museum's borders, in the process of forcibly removing museum holdings. This attack can be read as a counterattack, a counteroffensive in the battle to define art's role in communities. This art counterattack suggests art should not be "held" as a series of holdings, primarily accessible to a privileged few, but art should be free to move amongst the communities responsible for its production.

The Domino Affect

Similar to Mumbo Jumbo, The People of Paper features an artistic heterotopia of resistance. Federico de la Fe's living room, especially around the dominoes table, is transformed into a liberatory site.[38] As the insurgent leader's daughter, Little Merced frequently sees her domestic space, specifically, her family dominoes table, become the center for resistance organizing and strategizing. "My father sat bent over the dominoes table sketching plans and chewing the leaves of his tea. Once the fungus receded back into flower fields, the daily games of dominoes resumed. Froggy made Sandra subcomandante of EMF and, as subcomandante, Sandra sat next to Froggy . . . They would sit and study the charts that my father had drawn . . . 'Here is where we attack,' my father said."[39]

Throughout The People of Paper, Federico de la Fe's living room dominoes table is a nexus between organizing and culture. In many Latin American and Caribbean countries, and by extension, many Latinx and Caribbean communities in the United States, playing dominoes is a significant form of cultural expression.[40] The dominoes table is an affective cultural site for community building and for intra-family folkways and mores exchange. Stories and feelings are shared over dominoes. In Latin American and Caribbean communities, dominoes is often referred to as an art form or a sport (in Cuba, after baseball, dominoes is referred to as the "Second National Pastime."[41] Skilled practitioners of the art form, in some communities, are known as "dominologists."[42] Federico de la Fe uses dominoes art as a cultural technology to gain the trust of EMF gang members (and put them at ease) as he lays out insurgency plans. Dominoes have cultural currency. Since EMF community members share a familiarity with the art form and its cultural relevancy, using the dominoes table as a strategizing site subtly but powerfully creates a feeling of comfort for the community liberatory work at hand.

The domino table use is an affective and effective leadership move by Federico de la Fe because he is not originally from El Monte. The revolutionary leader's use of the game communicates the same message that Subcomandante Sandra communicated to Federico de la Fe's daughter Little Merced during her first menstruation: "See, I'm just like you." This leadership strategy can be an affective and effective organizing model off the page as well. When activists and organizers can root liberatory work in affective, culturally relevant activities and sites, it can do a kind of emancipatory work that even the most sophisticated organizing technologies cannot match. Strategy sessions in neighborhood barber shops and beauty salons, information sharing meetings before Friday night bingo, and recruitment outreach before soccer and basketball league play would all align with Federico de la Fe's use of the dominoes table as culturally relevant, liberatory technologies. Community organizers introducing emancipatory ideas to the community in the aforementioned ways are also sending an underlying message: "See, I'm just like you."

2

Heroes and Hieroglyphics of the Flesh in *The Salt Eaters* and *Heroes and Saints*

Embodied Hieroglyphics

Chapter 1 argues that ankhing's privileging of community folkways, Spirit, and art contribute to the elevation of Latinx and African-American animacy. Chapter 2 examines how sovereign representatives focus on attacking Brown and Black bodies, especially Brown and Black activist bodies, as a way to systematically subvert the collective animacy of Brown and Black communities. In this chapter, the imbricated relationship between ankhing and counterpublics is explored as a generative way to resist attacks on Brown and Black communities by engendering environments where animacy can be nurtured.

Toni Cade Bambara's *The Salt Eaters* begins with an interrogative rooted in flesh and soul: "Are you sure, sweetheart, that you want to be well?" At the radical Southwest Community Infirmary, local healer Minnie Ransom poses this wellness question to activist Velma Henry, who has recently tried to destroy her flesh by sticking her head in an oven. Distinguishing between "body" and "flesh," Hortense Spillers defines the flesh as "concentrated ethnicity" that has "zero degree of social conceptualization."[1] Pushed toward the "frontiers of survival,"[2] bare life, the African female subject is "a target of rape—in one sense, an interiorized violation of body and mind—but also the topic of specifically externalized acts of torture and prostration that we imagine as the peculiar province of male brutality and torture inflicted by other males."[3] Velma Henry's head in the oven is a disturbing signifier of an interiorized violation of body and mind, a manifest sign of internalized micro and macro aggressions. These aggressions leave Velma Henry's flesh wounded, marked with "hieroglyphics of the flesh."[4] Fleshly hieroglyphics, racialized disjunctures, are not always visible to the naked eye; they are often hidden by skin and history. Hieroglyphics of the flesh stealthily travel beneath the color line, a bloodletting Underground Railroad connecting African female bodies past and present. Spillers avers:

> These undecipherable markings on the captive body render a kind of hieroglyphics of the flesh whose severe disjunctures come to be hidden to the cultural seeing by skin color. We might well ask if this phenomenon of marking and branding actually 'transfers' from one generation to another, finding its various *symbolic substitutions* in an efficacy of meanings that repeat the initiating moments.[5]

Velma Henry's self-harming move toward the oven can be read as a symbolic substitution for hand-me-down ancestral pain: an outward articulation of transferable internalized oppression. Alexander Weheliye addresses and complicates oppression's transferability (in the context of the putatively liberated subject) by arguing, "'hieroglyphics of the flesh' . . . [are] transmitted to the succeeding generations of black subjects who have been 'liberated' and granted body in the aftermath of de jure enslavement. The hieroglyphics of the flesh do not vanish once affixed to proper personhood (the body); rather they endure as a pesky potential vital to the maneuverings of 'cultural seeing by skin color.'"[6]

Hieroglyphics of the flesh's dangerous resilience in Black and Brown communities creates a need for spatial resistance: counterpublics dedicated to resisting external and interiorized oppression. Fraser opines "[M]embers of subordinated social groups—women, workers, people of color, gays, and lesbians—have repeatedly found it advantageous to constitute alternative publics . . . where members of subordinated social groups invent and circulate counterdiscourses which in turn permit them to formulate oppositional interpretations of their identities, interests and needs."[7]

As a complement to Fraser's counterpublic analysis, it may be helpful to reiterate Squires's counterpublic goals: "foster resistance; test arguments and strategies in wider publics; create alliances; persuade outsiders to change views; perform public resistance to oppressive laws and social codes; gain allies."[8] Building on Fraser, Squires, and Foucault, Kohn's heterotopia of resistance notion argues for counterpublics as "sites for political emancipation; their function is social transformation."[9] In *The Salt Eaters*, Clybourne's Black residents need to create an emancipatory "alternative public" because of the external and interiorized threat of hieroglyphics of the flesh. Resisting hieroglyphics of the flesh is revolutionary: it demands a societal transformation vis-à-vis embodied Black matter. Resisting hieroglyphics of the flesh is choosing heightened animacy, choosing life, choosing *bios*.

Resisting Grapes of Wrath

In Cherríe Moraga's play *Heroes and Saints*, McLaughlin residents choose *bios* by choosing to create a heterotopia of resistance. Fictional McLaughlin intersects with the tragic nonfiction elements of McFarland, a San Joaquin Valley farming community near California Highway 99.[10] In the text, pesticide is dropped from crop duster planes late at night, then chemicals waft down upon rows and rows of grape groves. Early morning, rows and rows of farm workers pick grapes in the freshly sprayed grape fields. Pregnant women labor in these pesticide fields too. New mothers' newborn children begin to bear witness to the ravages of the "profit-over-people" neoliberal imperative underlying "Big Ag," corporate America's agriculture business interests. Bodies are born flesh. Babies are born with no arms and legs. The babies who emerge intact die too soon of cancers and other ailments that should not befall children. Mothers of McLaughlin, a grassroots activist group holds a politically and economically dangerous news conference to demand humane and honorable dealings between farm owners and farm workers. At the rally, the mothers risk losing jobs their families cannot afford to lose. The mothers stand up for their children. Mothers hold signs with succinct stories on them and read aloud their loss narratives:

AMPARO: Sandy Pérez. Died August 1, 1982. Ailment: acute Leukemia. Age 9.

MOTHER: Frankie Gonzales. Died March 16, 1986. Ailment: bone cancer. Age 10.

MOTHER: Johnny Rodríguez. Died July 10, 1987. Ailment: adrenal gland tumor. Age 5.

MOTHER: Rosalinda Lorta. Died June 5, 1980. Ailment: chest muscle tumor. Age 5.

MOTHER: Maira Sánchez. Died. August 30, 1987. Ailment: pituitary tumor. Age 6.

MOTHER: Mario Bravo. Died November 26, 1987. Ailment: cancer of the liver. Age 14.

MOTHER: Memo Delgado. Died October 24, 1988. Ailment: adrenal gland tumor. Age 6.

YOLANDA: Evalina Valle. Died November 2, 1989. Ailment: . . . ailment . . . era mi hija . . . era . . . mi hija![11]

The mothers' public resistance to their children's bodies turned flesh, resistance to their children pushed beyond the borders of bare life unto death, is a turning point in McLaughlin's sociopolitical trajectory. The fall of their children moves the mothers to collectively rise up and push back against communal hieroglyphics of the flesh. The mothers are seeking transformation of their lives and transformation of society itself. The transformation is rooted in the fields. In *Heroes and Saints*, the fields where the farm laborers live and work are transformed into an alternative public, a counterpublic where counterdiscourses are circulated and counterhegemonic ideas are developed: a heterotopia of resistance.

In addition to functioning as sites for political emancipation and societal transformation, Kohn argues that heterotopias of resistance are sites that foster "oppositional practices by sheltering counterhegemonic ideas and identities." In the fields, McLaughlin farm workers begin to develop the counterhegemonic idea that they deserve to be treated with dignity, respect, and concern for their health, despite their relative powerlessness vis-à-vis farm owners. Consistent with Ong's understanding of American neoliberalism, when profiteering farm owners drop death-dealing pesticides on the grape fields, this practice signifies that agriculture capitalists do not place much value on Latinx life, apart from its functionality as a profit-producing commodity.

The primarily Latinx McLaughlin community's cancer rates and birth defects (which seem linked to farm owners' discriminatory attitudes and policies) drive concerned neighbor Doña Amparo into action. Amparo is a factory worker and inhabitant of the federally subsidized housing that abuts the grape fields. Like *The People of Paper*'s farming community member Federico de la Fe, Amparo decides to foster resistance among her neighbors. Amparo hopes her neighbors will assist her in challenging a sovereign who is trying to delimit farm workers' lives.

Amparo's strategy involves getting her neighbors to see the environmental racism as a direct attack on the community's children. Despite signs that the local drinking water is unsafe, the school board refuses an offer from the water company, Arrowhead, to provide free drinking water for the local elementary school attended by McLaughlin farm workers' children. Amparo organizes a press conference at the elementary school. The TV news reporter, Ana Perez, sets the scene and summarizes the environmental racism claims:

> ANA PEREZ: A crowd is beginning to form out here in front of McLaughlin's elementary school. Mostly mothers and other neighbors have shown up this morning. There is no sign of school officials as of yet. Local residents are outraged by the school board's decision to refuse Arrowhead's offer of free drinking water for the school children. They believe the local tap water, contaminated by pesticides, to be the chief cause of the high incidence of cancer among the children in the area. They claim that the extensive spraying, especially aerial spraying, causes the toxic chemicals to seep into the public water system. The majority of residents are from a nearby housing tract of federally-subsidized housing. It has been alleged that the housing was built on what was once a dump site for pesticides with the full knowledge of contractors.[12]

Amparo procures a "cancer map" and begins to share the map with neighbors to inspire a resistance movement against the environmental racism plaguing their community:

> AMPARO: I'm sorry hija. (beat.) Vente. Quiero enseñarles algo.

YOLANDA: Que?

AMPARO: Hice un mapa. (She unrolls the chart onto the table.) A chart of all the houses in la vecindad que tiene gente con health problems.

YOLANDA: Let me see.

AMPARO: Miren, the red dots mean those houses got someone with cancer. Estos puntos azules donden tienen tumors. Los green ones son para birth defects y los amarillos, the miscarriages.

YOLANDA: What are all these orange dots?

AMPARO: Bueno, smaller problems como problemas del estómago, las ronchas, cosas así.

YOLANDA: Cheezus, it's the whole damn neighborhood.

CEREZITA: Where's our house?

AMPARO: Aquí donde están the orange dot and the green dot.

CEREZITA: That's me, the green dot.[13]

It is significant that Amparo chooses the State-owned, State-controlled, and State-administered elementary school as a site to foster resistance. Like the federally subsidized housing in which most of the farm workers live, the text suggests that the elementary school abuts the fields as well. There is no significant boundary between the fields where Brown farm workers labor, the housing where Brown farm workers live, and the schools where farm workers' Brown children are educated. The fluidity between these fields-centered sites indicates that the farm owners, supported by the State, circumscribe Brown farm workers' identities, hailing them as objects in the service of farm owner profits. Objectified, farm workers' dignity, health, and agency are subverted. This quality of life subversion is made manifest in the McLaughlin

School Board's refusal to accept clean drinking water for the farm workers' children. This is a State-endorsed refusal to fully value the lives of farm worker children and a State-sanctioned policy that makes tangible the belief that Brown children do not matter, that Brown matter does not matter.

The strategic press conference, featuring farm worker mothers narrating their loss, is an attempt to do what Squires argues counterpublics must do: persuade outsiders to change their views and gain allies. The process of persuading outsiders to change their views begins with the insiders. Subjects organized inside the counterpublic who are resisting the hegemonic gaze also must resist the hegemon's power to influence self-perception. The counterpublic insiders have to sufficiently resist hieroglyphics of the flesh's inner workings to *persuade themselves* that their lives are worth the risk-taking that liberatory labor demands. Community members must urgently persuade themselves to resist negative self-images. *Now.* The counterpublic qua heterotopia of resistance allows the oppressed to resist in the delimited now; the nowness of bare life can create an urgency where subjects can resist in the now as an investment toward future freedoms. Similarly, in Weheliye's discussion about the intersection of law and flesh, he contends that "habeas viscus unearths the freedom that exists within hieroglyphics of the flesh. For the oppressed the future will have been now, since Man tucks away this group's present."[14] The counterpublic-inspired press conference, in the now, coheres with Squires's counterpublic goal of performing public resistance. Public resistance is an evolutionary stage in counterpublic liberatory labor. After emancipatory strategies and theoretical frameworks have been adjudicated and decided upon in the subaltern counterpublic safe haven, the public expression of these decisions (i.e., public resistance) is what transforms liberatory activism from theory to praxis.

Sovereign Silence: Silent but Deadly

Public resistance is a freedom response to the disciplining nature of silence, a silence tethered to the sovereign's hegemonic gaze. As Derrida argues, sovereign power is "silent as it is unavowable. Silent and unavowable like Sovereignty itself. Unavowable silence, denegation: that is the always unapparent essence of sovereignty."[15] In *Heroes and*

Saints, when the McLaughlin School Board qua sovereign representative decides to reject Arrowhead's offer of clean drinking water for the elementary school children, the sovereign is disavowing the apparent reality that the area's well water is contaminated, negating that the birth defects are related to dangerous pesticide use. When the Mothers of McLaughlin break their silence and publicly speak out during the press conference, they are attacking the very "essence of sovereignty." This public resistance in response to bare life and death is a power move that imbricates with Lorde's contention about the intersection of silence and death:

> To question or to speak as I believed could have meant pain, or death. But all the hurt in so many ways, all the time, and pain will either change or end. Death on the other hand is the final silence. And that might be coming quickly, now, without regard for whether I had ever spoken what needed to be said, or had only betrayed myself into small silences, while I planned someday to speak, or waited for someone else's words. And I began to recognize a source of power within myself that comes from the knowledge . . . I was going to die, if not sooner then later, whether or not I had ever spoken. My silences had not protected me. Your silence will not protect you."[16]

Motivated by the death of their children, the Mothers of McLaughlin align with Lorde and resist disciplinary silence and name the death-dealing silent sovereign in the process. The children's analogous causes of death speak to the strong possibility of a common cause of death. By breaking their silence to narrate and name their loss narratives, the mothers make apparent the previously unapparent essence of sovereignty. In testifying to the deadly nature of the sovereign (along with its silent nature), the mothers are uttering the forbidden, engaging in discursive indiscretion. Foucault contends that "Silence itself—the thing one declines to say, or is forbidden to name, the discretion that is required between different speakers—is less the absolute limit of discourse, the other side from which it is separated by a strict boundary, than an element that functions alongside the things said."[17]

Much like McLaughlin's boundary between work sites and domestic sites, the McLaughlin's boundary is porous between what is said and what is forbidden to say. It is forbidden for farm workers to say that their employers' neoliberal practices are killing their children, but their children's bare life bodies speak through their mother's lips: hieroglyphics of the flesh turn grieving mothers into ventriloquists of the flesh.

It is dangerous to name sovereign death-dealers and to articulate the ways in which they distribute death. In the corporate agriculture, neoliberal context, making the sovereign visible can cost a person their livelihood or their life. Speaking out against Big Business is risky business. Throughout *Heroes and Saints*, the specter of sovereign violence is represented by the farm owners' armed men, patrolling the grape fields in low-flying helicopters. The porous boundaries between the fields, farm workers' homes, and the sovereign's sky makes the domestic sphere a place of anxiety. The aforementioned anxiety is illustrated during a protest rally in the fields outside of subsidized-housing resident Dolores's window:

> CEREZITA: Mira 'amá. They're all going house to house, giving out pamphlets. Father Juanito's there and Don Gilberto. They even got the news cameras.
>
> DOLORES: Get your face out of the window.
>
> CEREZITA: Nobody's looking over here.
>
> DOLORES: Quítate de allí, te digo.
>
> DOLORES *disengages* CEREZITA'S *raite and moves her away from the window.*
>
> CEREZITA: Ah, 'amá!
>
> DOLORES: Pues, you don't know who could be out there. All this protesta is bringing the guns down from the sky.[18]

Throughout the play, Dolores's reticence to engage the sovereign (due to concerns regarding her family's physical and economic well-being) operates as a counterbalance to resident-turned-activist Amparo's engagement with the sovereign. The juxtaposition of these two residents de-romanticizes liberation work, while highlighting the very real dangers involved when relatively less powerful subjects participate in liberatory labor. The nuanced differences between these Latina McLaughlin residents humanizes their individual struggles and dismantles simplistic characterizations of the working-poor.

Of Women and Heroes

From the safe distance of time, space, or more resourced subject position, it is not difficult to criticize some disenfranchised subjects for not standing up for their rights—especially when disenfranchised subjects around them are engaging in courageous emancipatory work. Dolores's children often praise Amparo for her activist work and wonder why their mother doesn't exhibit the same passion for engaging the sovereign. Dolores's retort speaks to the intersection of domestic composition and economic realities.

> DOLORES (*entering*): Es una metiche, Amparo.
>
> YOLANDA: They shot through her windows last night.
>
> CEREZITA: Who?
>
> YOLANDA: Who knows? The guys in helicopters . . .
>
> DOLORES: Por eso, te diga [AMPARO] better learn to keep her damn mouth shut. Ella siempre gottu be putting la cuchara en la olla. I saw her talk to the TV peepo last week right in front of the house.
>
> YOLANDA: What are you scared of?
>
> DOLORES: They come to talk to Amparo on the job yesterday.
>
> MARIO: Who?
>
> DOLORES: The patrones.

MARIO: The owners?

DOLORES: Not the owners, pero their peepo. They give her a warning that they don' like her talking about the rancheros.

YOLANDA: Cabrones.

DOLORES: She gointu lose her job.

MARIO: Got to hand it to Nina Amparo. She's got huevos, man.

DOLORES: She got a husband, not huevos. Who's gointu support Cere if I stop working?[19]

Dolores's perspective is informed by a problematic heteronormative understanding of family construction. Yet, beneath this problematic construction lies the economic insecurity tethered to working-poor households relying on one income. Losing a job can be catastrophic when there is no partner to fill the gap. This economic reality is heightened when dependent children are factored into the equation. The aforementioned scene signifies the irony throughout *Heroes and Saints*: when the dispossessed defend their children against the sovereign, they risk endangering their children's welfare at the hands of the sovereign. The confluence of injustice, economic conditions, child welfare, and activism necessitates a more nuanced understanding of what constitutes a hero. Amparo can be considered a liberatory figure given the ways in which she risks (and eventually loses) her job to protest her community's mistreatment. Identifying Dolores's choices as emancipatory requires closer examination, especially when juxtaposed against Amparo's actions.

Dolores frames Amparo's activism as a process of constantly placing "la cuchara en la olla," putting her "spoon in the pot." Dolores's use of this idiomatic expression suggests that she believes Amparo is creating problems for the community by "stirring up trouble." Amparo is alarmed that Dolores spoke with the "TV peepo last week right in front of [her] house." Dolores is concerned that her house, and her familial inhabitants, will be tethered to Amparo's attempts to avow the unavowable actions of the silent sovereign through the media. Dolores wants to silence Amparo; she wants Amparo to "learn to keep her damn mouth shut." "Learn," the education verb's use is significant. According to Dolores, Amparo hasn't embraced the sovereign's educational dictates, which entail embracing a bare life subject position. Amparo hasn't accepted the sovereign's lesson about McLaughlin's Latinx community's relative powerlessness, which makes engaging the relatively powerful sovereign a futile exercise. How can Amparo's actions be liberatory, especially when they represent a direct affront to Dolores's more readily apparent liberatory actions?

In the passage above, Dolores enters the room and learns that someone has shot bullets through the window into Amparo's family home. Certainly, a terrifying act given the narrative's repeated references to death-dealing armed men in helicopters, who patrol and fire at the sovereign's behest. The play's short opening scene (which features no dialogue) ends with the "sound of a low-flying helicopter invad[ing] the silence. Its shadow passes over the field."[20] It seems apparent that Dolores is well aware of McLaughlin's clear and present dangers. Yet, when Yolanda asks Dolores (in the passage above), "What are you scared of?" Dolores's answer doesn't mention helicopters, guns, bullets, or shattered windows. Instead, Dolores answers with: "They come to talk to AMPARO on the job yesterday." Dolores's job concerns are trumped by her violence concerns. This duty-bound decision to protect her job is rooted in her children's welfare. Dolores's husband deserted the family, narrowing her capacity for risk-taking as the sole familial economic supporter. Dolores is defending her family's long-term prospects by securing her job's long-term prospects. This economic-based motivation is illuminated by the interrogative that ends the passage: "Who's gointu support Cere if I stop working?" For Dolores, safeguarding her child's survival with agricultural labor *is* liberatory labor.

In the passage above, Dolores juxtaposes her understanding of liberatory labor with Amparo's understanding of liberatory labor. Unlike her children, Dolores does not think that her approach to emancipatory labor is less valid than Amparo's approach. In fact, Dolores is critical of Amparo's emancipatory labor, because she feels Amparo is a *metiche*, or "busy body," whose pot stirring may create problems (due to affiliation) for her at work—or through her windows. After Amparo shows Dolores the cancer map, chronicling the carcinogenic impact of Big Agriculture's neoliberal policies, Dolores snatches the map from Amparo and says, "This is the las' time I'm gointu say it, I don' wan' this biznis in my house."[21] Activist Amparo's response to Dolores is noteworthy. Amparo's response gives insight to her approach to organizing and also ends Scene One: "DOLORES throws the chart out the door and goes back to feeding CEREZITA, shoving the food into her mouth. AMPARO leaves in silence. Fade out."[22] Amparo's silent response tacitly acknowledges the validity of Dolores's liberatory labor strategy. Amparo's silence operates as a discourse strategy. Amparo doesn't have to agree with Dolores's approach nor does she have to demonize Dolores for not engaging the sovereign with direct action. Amparo understands that there are many silences and many discourse strategies for engaging multitudinous silences. Similarly, Foucault argues, "There is not one but many silences, and they are an integral part of the strategies that underlie and permeate discourses."[23] Amparo's silent response to Dolores also functions as an embrace of alterity.

Creating a heterotopia of resistance in the fields, with its porous borders between work and domestic spaces, necessitates valuing alterity. Amparo understands that difference is a resource. Kohn suggests that heterotopias of resistance are "safe havens" for ideas that privilege democratic styles of information-sharing, while functioning as safe havens for subjects (and their ideas), who may represent difference *within* heterotopias of resistance. Alterity is not only acknowledged, but also seen as a source of epistemological value and a resource for the effective implementation of collectively derived strategies.[24] In the McLaughlin fields qua heterotopias of resistance, Amparo's and Dolores's different strategic, emancipatory approaches enhance the epistemological possibilities within the fields: their alterity is a resource that engenders liberatory best practices. Amparo's strategic silence to Dolores coheres with the second element in the ankhing process in that it supports efforts to collectively think through the most effective means to resist hegemonic forces—and through this idea-exchange, inspire, motivate, and move each other toward liberatory best practices.

Amparo's silent response doesn't alienate Dolores. The response is not judgmental. Instead, Amparo's strategic silence empowers Dolores to stand strong in her own child-centered, "immediate material needs" approach to liberatory labor. Furthermore, this non-judgmental discourse strategy provides Dolores self-interrogation space to evolve to a position where she can honor her family's immediate material needs *and* directly engage the sovereign. Self-interrogation and intra-counterpublic evolution need to be critical elements in heterotopias of resistance. Effective emancipatory counterpublics should have deeply embedded, inward-focused interrogation concerning the ways in which the group creates, develops, and adjudicates epistemological approaches and liberatory practices. This type of intra-counterpublic evolution is important, because emancipatory internal structures and emancipatory internal systems are not static—especially under the totalizing, atomizing gaze of a neoliberal force.

The McLaughlin fields' non-static nature is what eventually provides Dolores with the impetus to self-interrogate, leading to her liberatory approach's evolution. The increasing numbers of putatively pesticide-related deaths begins to radicalize McLaughlin's Latinx community members, including people close to Dolores. As a powerful protest act, unnamed community members begin to disinter Latinx children's corpses and hang them from wooden crucifixes in the grape fields.[25]

Following the pesticide-related death of Evalina Valle, Dolores's infant granddaughter, the Latinx community is outraged. Community members walk toward grape fields in Evalina's public funeral procession carrying photos of their own dead and disabled children.[26] Dolores's armless and legless daughter Cerezita (who in the preceding scene has a transfiguration-like experience where she is transformed into a manifestation of la Virgen de Guadalupe[27]) addresses the funeral procession:

> Put your hand inside my wound . . . You are the miracle people because today, this day, that red memory will spill out from inside you and flood this valley con coraje. And you will be free. Free to name this land *Madre*. Madre Tierra. Madre Sagrada. Madre . . . Libertad.[28]

Combining the la Virgen de Guadalupe transfiguration scene with the scene above, Cerezita is evolving from a victim of neoliberal-driven environmental racism to an inspiring community activist fighting against neoliberal-driven environmental racism—while representing and embodying a radical political role for the culturally conservative Catholic icon la Virgen de Guadalupe. Yvonne Yarbo-Bejarano's perspective coheres with this study's analysis: "Cere infuses the traditional [la Virgen de Guadalupe] image with the secular and the political. In *Heroes*, religion provides the vehicle for a vision of an alternative syncretic practice fusing activism and spirituality that complements the text's critique of institutional Catholicism."[29] By fusing activism and spirituality, Cerezita gives voice to bare life by speaking from bare life—and in the process moving away from the margins of life. The speaking (and self-defining) subject moves away from objecthood. Objectified subjects shape-shift when they center themselves.

In their response to environmental racism, the mothers function as ventriloquists of the flesh, speaking for their bare life children. When Cerezita says, "Put your hand inside my wound," she is not only speaking for herself, but also connecting her own suffering to her community's suffering. However, Cerezita does not dwell in victimhood. Instead, she hails her fellow community members as "miracle people," who have the agency to turn their hardship history ("red memory") into courage ("coraje"). Cerezita calls for the McLaughlin community members to evolve into new subject positions defined by the courage to seek and speak emancipation from the sovereign's delimiting silent yoke, to seek and speak "libertad."

Dolores is present for Cerezita's speech. Witnessing her daughter's public step into community activism opens Dolores to a more direct engagement with the sovereign. The local Catholic priest Father Juan and Cerezita want Yolanda (Dolores's daughter) to offer her dead infant's body (Evalina) as a ritual crucifixion in the grape fields:

> They both turn to YOLANDA. YOLANDA now understands that she is to offer up her dead infant. She goes to the coffin, takes it from the altar boys, kisses it, then hands it over to Juan.[30]

Throughout the play, Dolores had aggressively dissuaded her children from any form of anti-sovereign activism; however, Dolores does not intervene when Yolanda hands over Evalina (Dolores's granddaughter) for crucifixion as a protest against the death-dealing sovereign. Furthermore, Dolores does not intervene when her godchild Bonnie brings to Father Juan the wooden cross that is to be used for the crucifixion. Even when it becomes clear that Cerezita will be accompanying Father Juan to the grape fields for the protest crucifixion, Dolores does not intercede. Instead, when Cerezita is about to pass Dolores on her way to the grape fields with Father Juan, Dolores makes a gesture that signifies her evolving political consciousness:

> CEREZITA pauses briefly as she passes her mother.
>
> CEREZITA: Mamá.
>
> DOLORES blesses her. CEREZITA and JUAN proceed offstage into the vineyards.[31]

In the above passage, Dolores gives her "blessing" to Cerezita's desire to engage in direct action and protest the neoliberal farm owners' death-dealing practices. This verbal gesture aligns Dolores with the McLaughlin Mothers who avowed the unavowable on behalf of their bare life children. Through utterance, Dolores is making the transition into direct action against the neoliberal farm owners.

Sovereign-sponsored violence engenders Dolores's evolution into direct engagement with the sovereign. Just after Juan and Cerezita reach the grape fields for the ritual crucifixion "the shadow and sound of a helicopter pass overhead . . . Then there is the sudden sound of machine gun fire."[32] Throughout the play, Dolores is concerned that the appearance of being affiliated with the resistance movement would make her children targets of sovereign violence. In particular, Dolores worries about the armed men in helicopters who patrol the borderless fields. Dolores is distressed enough by the possibility of violence that she prevents her children from standing next to her house's windows. Cerezita is with Father Juan in the grape fields, so the machine gun fire is representative of Dolores's worst fears. Initially, Dolores (and the other Latinx community members) scream in terror, drop to the ground and cover their heads. Suddenly, Dolores's son Mario rises, raises his fist, and shouts, "Burn the fields"![33] Dolores (and the other community members) rise with Mario and begin to shout, "enciendan los files!" Dolores and the McLaughlin residents rush out to the vineyards screaming, "Asesinos!" or "murderers!"

It is significant that "asesinos" is the play's last word of dialogue (it is repeated three times), and it is significant that Dolores (among other Latinx community members) is chanting "murderers." Dolores is verbally identifying the farm owners qua sovereign as death-dealers.

Dolores is avowing the unavowable about the death-dealer who operates in silence and whose power is undergirded by intimidating people into silence. By the play's end, Dolores has evolved from using a liberatory strategy that uses silence to support her children to a liberatory strategy that breaks silence to support her children. Dolores's evolution to direct action against the sovereign does not invalidate her prior strategy in protecting her job to protect her children. In heterotopias of resistance, strategic best practices are not based on either/or paradigms. Since emancipatory internal structures and emancipatory internal systems are not static, strategic best practices are not static. In the McLaughlin fields, with its socioeconomic and physical dangers, and its porous borders between private domestic spaces and public work spaces, a heterotopia of resistance situated in this fluid context must be fluid. Dolores's strategic evolution is indicative of this fluidity.

Amparo's non-demonizing response to Dolores's initial "silence strategy" aligns with the ankhing approach, which privileges alterity, diverse ideas, and democratic decision making. By not attacking Dolores's non-engagement with the sovereign, Amparo avails Dolores the opportunity to evolve at her own pace, dictated by her own material conditions, and the specific circumstances within her own family unit. During the play's action, Dolores's family conditions dramatically change, inclusive of: her grandchild Evalina's pesticide-related death, Cerezita's radicalization, Cerezita's direct sovereign engagement and Cerezita's apparent murder in the grape fields. These material changes necessitate a radical change in Dolores's liberatory strategy that is more closely aligned with Amparo's emancipatory strategy concerning community activism. As the ankhing process suggests, Amparo's embrace of alterity and diverse ideas, versus an autocratic, top-down leadership style, proves to be a more efficacious way to encourage community members to engage in direct action against the sovereign.

From Page to Pavement to Politics of the Spirit

Amparo's approach with Dolores can be a model for real-world community activists. There is a problematic community organizer tradition whereby activists relate as the experts on community problems (as opposed to community members being the experts about their own communities).³⁴ This tradition can be exacerbated if the organizers have putatively more "sophisticated" theoretical and ideological underpinnings than the folk they are attempting to organize.

However, this study is not arguing against organizers having a command of progressive theoretical and ideological epistemologies to frame their motivations and approaches to community activism. Generally, progressive theoretical and ideological epistemologies can be productive technologies in community activism when they are employed in ways that are not condescending, which is to say, when they are employed in ways that do not disrespect site-specific and cultural-specific epistemologies of the communities that are being organized. Amparo's engagement with Dolores is rooted in respect—which is why it proves productive. In community activism, respect is an extremely useful technology. The *Heroes and Saints* narrative is a repository of possibilities for examining how respect functions in effective community activism. The play's fictive narrative can function as a resource for activists who are interested in thinking creatively about how to signal respect for the individuals and communities they are helping to organize.

Spirituality is another technology found in fictive *Heroes and Saints* that can serve as a repository for real-world effective activism. Earlier in this study, Kohn argues that heterotopias of resistance employ the Spirit as a technology to encourage liberatory subjects' emotions, because emotion is a source of power. Like Kohn, Cone believes resistance sites need to be spaces where people can "feel the Spirit." Both theorists suggest that subjects need to feel a passion for their cause. Since the Spirit-fueled sensorium plays a critical role in emancipatory labor, spirituality or religion does not have to function as the "opiate of the masses." The "dichotomy between the spiritual and the political is also false," as Lorde argues.³⁵ If there is a false dichotomy between the spiritual and the political, is there a possibility that there can be a productive relationship between the spiritual and the political?

In *Heroes and Saints*, the relationship between the spiritual and the political is both productive and contradictory. Throughout the text, Dolores is represented as a religious woman who places her liberatory hopes in God, while Amparo is represented, primarily, as a woman who places her hopes in activism. These designations are seen when the women are repairing Dolores's crumbling house in the early morning:

DOLORES: This house is falling apart. Ayúdanos, Dios!

AMPARO: You think God is gointu take care of it? Working is what changes things, not oraciones.

DOLORES: Ye te dije, I'm not going to your protesta.

AMPARO puts on the gloves, begins digging into the front yard. DOLORES goes over to the side of the house and starts applying plaster to it.

AMPARO: Sabes que? I don' even go to church no more, ni recibir communion . . . coz I'm tired of swallowing what they want to shove down my throat. Body of Christ . . . pedo.

DOLORES: I hate when you talk like this. It makes me sick to my stomach.[36]

Dolores's use of the phrase "Ayúdanos, Dios!" or "God help us!" is representative of her problem-solving approach. Though "oraciones," or "prayers," Dolores seeks God's help to deal with the negative externalities associated with living under the sovereign's hegemonic gaze. Dolores's prayers operate in her cosmology as direct action to engage her Sovereign who has dominion over the sovereign. Dolores's access to her Sovereign provides her access to an emancipatory technology more powerful than Amparo's brand of community activism. Dolores's social justice technology is powered my faith and prayer; it allows her to declare with conviction, "I'm not going to your protesta." For Dolores, a community protest against the sovereign not only places her family at risk, it places her family at risk, while lacking her Sovereign's liberatory power to respond to the risk.

For Amparo, the Sovereign resides inside the people and inside the labor the people produce. "Labor" and "inside" are the significant terms. Amparo's actions suggest a belief that McLaughlin community members must explore inside themselves until they come into communion with the part of the individual self that is sacred, the part of the self that is worth the risk inherent in directly engaging the neoliberal sovereign. In Amparo's cosmology, community activism labor is an expression of spirituality. Digging for truth about the hegemon's death-dealing practices is Amparo's way to defend and praise the indwelling Spirit of community members. While Dolores is plastering the outside of the house, Amparo is digging in the yard. Amparo digs up a rubber hose, unearthing the remains of a toxic waste dump their homes were built on. Despite excavating the truth, Dolores says, "No es nada." However, Amparo challenges her religious friend's disbelief: "You don' believe me, but they bury all of their poisons under our houses."[37] Dolores's faith is strong in the things unseen, but she struggles to believe in what can be seen—especially when what is seen is the death-dealing apparatus that confirms how little the neoliberal sovereign values her life—and the lives of her children.

As a bare life survival strategy, Dolores chooses to plaster over the sovereign-produced familial fissures: transforming the seen into the unseen for survival's sake. Amparo questions this survival strategy by framing it as an appeasement strategy:

> What you think that crack comes from? An earthquake? The house is sinking, te digo como quicksand . . . They lied to us, Lola. They thought we was too stupid to know the difference. They throw some dirt over a dump, put some casas de cartón on top of it y dicen que it's the "American Dream." Pues, this dream has turned to pesadilla."[38]

Amparo encourages Dolores to confront the reality before her eyes and beneath her feet. The sovereign is sinking McLaughlin community laborers, and their children, into a death-dealing heap of toxic waste. With the assertion, "They thought we was too stupid," Amparo appeals to Dolores's intelligence and dignity by framing the sovereign's actions as attacks on the community's intelligence and dignity. In the neoliberal context, the sovereign is selling a cleverly wrapped "American Dream," but the concealed contents include a poverty-wage job, unclean drinking water, and a rickety house built on a cancer-causing toxic waste site. According to Dolores, the sovereign assumes the immigrant Latinx workers will pay the grotesque price mark-up, because the mythic American Dream advertising campaign has been so effective. Without demonizing her, Amparo indirectly urges Dolores to reconsider her appeasement approach since the sovereign lied and sold them a crumbling pesadilla, or nightmare, wrapped in a shiny package.

The American Nightmare with the crumbling foundation Dolores is plastering can be read as a signifier for the family dwelling inside its unstable walls. Dolores's relationship with her son, Mario, is increasingly strained, because she can't accept the open secret that he is gay. When she finally confronts Mario, Dolores frames his sexual orientation as a crumbling of his "manhood" and an affront to her Sovereign:

DOLORES: God made you a man and you throw it away. You lower yourself into half a man.

MARIO: I don't want to fight 'amá. I'm leaving in the morning. Give me your blessing. Send me on my way with the sign of the cross and a mother's love.

DOLORES: No puedo.

MARIO: You don't have to approve of it, 'amá.

DOLORES: No puedo. Peepo like you are dying. They got thá sickness. How can I give mi bendición para una vida que te va a matar. God makes this sickness to show peepo it's wrong what they do. Díme que te vas a cambiar y te doy mi benediction. Tu eres el único macho. I want you to live.

MARIO: I want to live too. I can't make you see that. Your god's doing all the seeing for you.[39]

Informed by her understanding of God, Dolores asserts that same-gendered-loving men devolve down the human animacy hierarchical scale to the "lower" stratum inhabited by "half-men." However, for Dolores, these half-men aren't "half as alive" as heterosexual men; gay men slide so far down the human animacy scale toward bare life that Dolores doubts their desire to "want to live." Dolores avers that a same-gendered-love life is a life that "va a matar," a "life that is going to kill." More troubling, Dolores's Sovereign is the death-dealer.

Dolores's Sovereign created a death-dealing disease, AIDS, to show same-gendered-lovers that same-gendered-love is wrong. Dolores's Sovereign kills in the name of love—while it kills because of love.

The hegemonic reach of Dolores killer-Sovereign is so totalizing that it has the power to preempt a mother's love for her son. When Mario asks Dolores to send him on his journey with "the sign of the cross and a mother's love," she answers "no puedo," or "I can't." It is important to note that Dolores does not say, "I don't want to." The decision to love her son is removed from Dolores's purview. The decision is not an issue of choice: she can't. Dolores cannot love her gay son because only her Sovereign can decide for her whom to love. Dolores's Sovereign God speaks for her and decides which words cannot be uttered. As with the silent, sovereign farm owners, Dolores is silenced by her own Sovereign. As with the silent, sovereign farm owners, Dolores's Sovereign restricts her ability to undergird and protect her family: her Sovereign delimits her agency. Dolores cannot make the "sign of the cross," cannot confer a blessing in the name of love. Like Dolores's voice, her body is controlled. This bodily control is inclusive of Dolores's eyes—and the ways in which they view the world.

Dolores's Sovereign disallows her from seeing her son as fully human. Not only does Dolores see Mario as a partial man, she sees him as partially alive. Dolores tells Mario, "I want you to live," because her Sovereign-controlled vision sees him inhabiting a subjectivity near the lower stratum of life due to his sexual orientation. Dolores's Sovereign and the farm owner sovereign align in their perspectives on Mario. Both sovereigns push him down the human animacy scale and toward bare life. The neoliberal sovereign's downward thrust is primarily propelled by a toxic cocktail of class, race, and profiteering. Farm owners target the economically distressed, migrant Latinx workers because they are socially and politically vulnerable. In *Heroes and Saints*, politically and socioeconomically vulnerable subjects are easier to exploit since they typically have fewer political and socioeconomic resources to defend themselves against neoliberal farm owners. Mario's life course is delimited by the farm owners' death-dealing neoliberalism to such an extent that he is forced to seek liberation outside his hometown farming community's borders. The distance Mario seeks seems to stand in opposition to the family-oriented folkways that the narrative suggests are tethered to Latinx culture: folkways that promote intra-family physical and emotional proximity. Mario's desire to step outside these philosophical and physical boundaries, to choose life, requires a blessing from his mother—the giver of his life. Ultimately, Dolores cannot confer the blessing for life, because she has accepted the dictates of her Sovereign and the neoliberal sovereign who have both chosen death for the life that came though her.

Similar to the relationship between Amparo and Dolores, the relationship between Catholic priest Father Juan and Cerezita highlights the contradictory and productive relationship between the spiritual and the political. Father Juan is a proponent of liberation theology but not always an adherent to the theo-political philosophy that centers social justice for the dispossessed—and calls upon religious leaders to lead the justice charge.[40] As a Jesuit, Father Juan is forced to confront the dangers of liberation when news comes that six Salvadoran Jesuit priests (and their housekeeper and her daughter) have been murdered for defending the rights of the poor against the neoliberal sovereign. Fear for his own life makes Father Juan struggle to place his liberation theology philosophy into practice. In the narrative, Father Juan flees when the threat of sovereign violence emerges during direct actions being waged by McLaughlin residents against the neoliberal sovereign farm owners. Witnessing this pattern, Cerezita begins to engage Father Juan about his motivations and intentions:

CEREZITA: Why did you become a priest, Father Juan?

JUAN: Too many years as an altar boy . . . and because of the fabric.

CEREZITA: The fabric?

JUAN: Yes. Literally, the cloth itself drew me to be a "man of the cloth." The vestment, the priest's body asleep underneath that cloth, the heavy weight of it tranquilizing him.

CEREZITA: Will you always be a priest, Father Juan?

JUAN: There's no choice in the matter. Once ordained, you've given up volition in that sense. The priesthood is an indelible mark. You are bruised by it, not violently, but its presence is always felt. A slow dull ache, a slight discoloration in the skin . . .

∽

CEREZITA: But that's your job, isn't it, Father, to make people see? The 'theology of liberation.' The spiritual practice of freedom. On earth. Do you practice what you preach, Father?[41]

In the above passage, Cerezita challenges the contention that Father Juan can be both a liberation theology practitioner and a Sovereign representative. Responding to Cerezita's interrogatives, Father Juan confesses that the weight of the vestments is "tranquilizing" his body. A tranquilized body is unable to forcefully move into liberatory action when "the liberatory moment" calls for liberatory action. Throughout *Heroes and Saints*, Father Juan is defined by his inability to act on his purported liberation theology philosophy—especially in the liberatory moments when the McLaughlin community members need him most.

Father Juan explains to Cerezita that operating as an ordained Sovereign representative "there's no choice in the matter." Father Juan has "given up volition." The priest's will is not his own. Father Juan's will is owned by the Sovereign. Although his liberation theology philosophy dictates a moral, political, and philosophical imperative to help Cerezita, and the other McLaughlin youth who she has helped to organize against the sovereign farm owners, Father Juan's will falls short when it comes to carrying out emancipatory actions. Similar to Dolores's Sovereign-dictated refusal to bless Mario, Father Juan is the narrative's second adult "caregiver" to sacrifice children on the altar of "abdicated volition."

Whether religious or neoliberal, the sovereign impact on the McLaughlin youth is marked by violence. The neoliberal farm owners' death-dealing policies etch indelible violence in the shape of badly deformed bodies and bodies that never form into adults. In *Heroes and Saints*, religious Sovereign violence is less legible but not necessarily less violent. In the play, Sovereign violence has a way of working inside-out. Sovereign violence does damage by encouraging the host subject to do damage to him/herself—and to those in his or her care. Dolores allows the Sovereign working within her to stop the flow of maternal love toward her gay son because of who he chooses to love. The love Dolores denies Mario hurts him, but the harm to Dolores is palpable as well. Earlier in the play, before Dolores refuses to confer her blessings on Mario, she says about her children, "[Y]ou walk around full of holes from all the places they take from you. All the times you worry for them . . . all the times you see them suffer on their faces and your hands are tied down from helping them."[42] It is her Sovereign who ties down Dolores's hand from making the sign of the cross to bless her gay son. Consequently, it is her Sovereign who helps generate the invisible, non-legible "holes" that Dolores carries inside. However, these indwelling holes (hieroglyphics of the flesh) are not empty. These holes are occupied by a Sovereign who works inside-out. The Sovereign works from inside Dolores's consciousness by functioning *as* her subjectivity. The Sovereign convinces Dolores to *convince herself* that she must deny love to her son.

Father Juan claims that life as a Sovereign representative leaves an "indelible mark" that bruises, causes "a slight discoloration in the skin," but that it is not violent. Yet, Father Juan's inability to practice his liberation theology co-signs the continuation of neoliberal sovereign profiteering policies that mark Brown bodies as less valuable on the human animacy scale. Father Juan's sovereign appeasement policy, despite his claims, operates as violence against his own Brown body and McLaughlin's Brown bodies that he is charged with shepherding toward life. Co-signing death-dealing neoliberal policies manifests as an abdication of his spiritual father duties. Father Juan is not shepherding his flock toward life; he is allowing the neoliberal sovereign to push his flock to the edge of bare life. Similar to the way the Sovereign and the neoliberal sovereign align to control Dolores's actions, Father Juan's Sovereign and the neoliberal sovereign collaborate to put his "body asleep" underneath that cloth, the heavy weight of it tranquilizing him.

In the context of Father Juan abdicating his religious and political duties (as a proponent of liberation theology), activist Amparo functions as both hero and saint in *Heroes and Saints*. Amparo's elevation into a "saintly" figure is one of the play's most interesting intersections of the spiritual and the political. Throughout the play, Amparo is skeptical of religion (and its representatives) as a liberatory technology. Amparo's skepticism emerges in her response to Dolores's "Help us God" comment, while they are repairing Dolores's home (which can be read as a material signifier for the Latinx McLaughlin community): "You think God is gointu take care of it? Working is what changes things, not oraciones." The work-that-changes is the community activism that Amparo engages in throughout *Heroes and Saints*: the cancer education campaign, organizing via private conversations, publicly resisting corporate sovereign death-dealing practices, and speaking at protest rallies. Amparo's community organizing operates as salvific emancipatory labor. The activist promotes and models access to community salvation via organizing community members to save themselves. Amparo allows her body to suffer to mitigate the suffering of community members.

Amparo's activist-related suffering echoes the suffering of Jesus during the Passion. In Christian narratives, the Passion chronicles Jesus's suffering at the hands of the Roman State apparatus during his final days. The Passion starts with Jesus leading a peaceful, procession-like rally on his way toward Jerusalem and concludes with the Roman State apparatus breaking his body in the presence of his followers.[43] While speaking at a peaceful rally against the neoliberal sovereign, a policeman knocks Amparo down with his nightstick and proceeds to methodically beat her until her body is broken.

Following the beating:

DON GILBERTO brings AMPARO out in a wheelchair
She has a black eye and wears a hospital gown and carries
a small purse in her lap. . . .

AMPARO: They cut out my spleen. Father it was completely smash.

DON GILBERTO: . . . [The doctor] says that the spleen is the part of the body that 'stá connectado con el coraje.

JUAN: It's the place of emotion, of human passions.

AMPARO: Pues, that policia got another thing coming if he think he could take away mi passion.[44]

In the crises moment, when McLaughlin's children's bodies are suffering under the yoke of neoliberal profit-maximization, Amparo offers up her body to suffer on the front line of resistance. Amparo's black eye and broken spleen signify the community activist's stigmata. Bearing witness to children suffering in the name of profits changes the way Amparo views the world; it blackens her vision. Amparo's black eye, this mark of shame and violence, is also a Passion-like mark of honor. The Passion mark signifies a transformational figure's ability to transform dishonor (suffered in an act of service) into honor. In the Roman Catholic Passion narrative, Jesus's Passion marks on his hands, feet, and side are physical signifiers of his suffering for the community he is serving. In the Passion narrative, the marks are wounds of love.

Similar to Jesus's narrative, Amparo's black eye and crushed spleen tell a community love story. Amparo's passion for her community moved her to the front lines of liberatory action. The activist engages in her own Passion Play by leading a community procession to challenge the neoliberal sovereign's death-dealing policies. Amparo's public humiliation, including her body being broken, inspires numerous community members to commit to embracing Amparo's activist lifestyle. Amparo becomes a moral exemplar, who is able to (as Bennett reading Kant writes in the Introduction) "infect free beings and induce conduct resembling that of the exemplar." Amparo's liberatory-tethered sacrifice and suffering inspires community members to sacrifice and suffer in the name of liberation. Amparo helps to create a spiritual movement, rooted in activating the inner Spirit toward outward liberatory labor. Doña Amparo's edifying actions elevate her and (by their association) elevates activists into a salvific role in the McLaughlin community. Amparo's emancipatory actions inspire the Brown faithful to reject bare life even if means risking death.

Inspired by Amparo's courage, Father Juan, Cerezita, and Mario risk death to confront neoliberal death-dealers. Throughout most of the text, Father Juan consistently fails to align his liberation theology philosophy with his liberation theology lifestyle. However, after witnessing Amparo's body being broken for justice (and failing to intervene), Father Juan has a "come-to-Amparo" moment—which engenders courage in the face of oppression. Despite a warning that the farm owner, neoliberal representatives will open fire on anyone who enters the vineyards to engage in ritual protest, Father Juan decides to defy death to resist bare life.

BONNIE: Now, is the time Father?

> JUAN nods then takes the cross from her. Another child brings JUAN some rope. He goes to CEREZITA, touches her cheek and releases the locks on the raite . . . YOLANDA now understands that she is to offer up her dead infant. . . . JUAN and CEREZITA head out to the vineyard.[45]

Earlier in the text, when it was "time" for Father Juan to take a liberatory stand, he ran. In the passage above (which occurs after Amaparo's body is broken for taking a liberatory stand), Father Juan, "nods and takes the cross" when the time for emancipatory action arrives. As in the Jesus narrative, Father Juan accepts and "takes up his cross."

The cross is both a signifier for his liberatory responsibility to the McLaughlin community and a symbol for the ultimate price that he may have to pay for accepting the cross. Crucifying dead children in the vineyard (as ritual protest against neoliberal farm owners' death-dealing policies) has been strictly forbidden. Protesters violating the ban have been threatened with death-dealing bullets. Yet, Juan and Cerezita "head out to the vineyard." It is significant that Father Juan makes this salvific move towards the vineyard with Cerezita because in the same scene, "A brilliant beam of light has entered the room and washed over CEREZITA. She is draped in the blue-starred veil of La Virgen de Guadalupe . . . The cross rests at the base of the raite. The light, brighter now, completely illuminates CERE'S saint-like expression and the small cross."[46]

Similarly inspired by Amparo's activism, Cerezita transforms into a liberatory iteration of a Virgen de Guadalupe/Jesus hybrid (just before they go to the vineyard Cerezita echoes Jesus's narrative and says to the community, "Put your hand inside my wound"). When the reader/audience is introduced to Cerezita, her body is already broken. Cerezita's broken body haunts the text as an embodiment of neoliberalism's impact on McLaughlin's youth, McLaughlin's future. Cerezita tells individual community members to, "Put your hand inside my wound," because neoliberal farm owners' death-dealing policies have wounded the children, the future of McLaughlin—and the adults hold some responsibility for this turn of events. Cerezita is both indicting adults for past inaction and seeking to inspire adults toward future liberatory action. Cerezita is transforming her open wound into a liberatory portal. The child's open sore functions as an open mouth calling neighbors to enter and pick up their cross. The open wound speaks the unavowable; it breaks the silence that the neoliberal sovereign employs to stealthily deal death. Cerezita's embodied suffering names the perpetrator and provides the salvific pathway to resist the perpetrator and reject bare life. "Put your hand inside my wound" is the liberatory password: the password to the resistance fields.

Just before Cerezita and Father Juan enter the resistance fields to perform the protest ritual crucifixion, "Dolores blesses [Cerezita]." Dolores's ritual act to affirm her daughter's activist agency shows evolution from her inability to confer a blessing on her son's activist agency. Dolores was unable to bless Mario's agentic decision to escape bare life, because she couldn't resist her Sovereign's influence. However, after Amparo's salvific suffering, Dolores is able to resist the neoliberal sovereign and her own Sovereign's influence and bless Cerezita's direct action against the purveyors of bare life—even though the death-dealers have threatened death to those entering the fields. Dolores makes a transition to an ideological position that asserts that resisting bare life is worth risking life. This ideological shift is a critical step in agentic liberatory evolution, because it presupposes a higher position on the animacy scale than the disenfranchised subject's sociopolitical standing would indicate. Brown life matters enough to die in its defense.

Moments after Father Juan and Cerezita enter the resistance fields, with Dolores's blessing, "the shadow and sound of a helicopter pass over head . . . then there is a sudden sound of machine gun fire . . . Mario suddenly rises, raises his fist into the air."[47] Following Amparo, Father Juan and Cerezita's salvific moves, Mario makes a strategic shift. Mario marks this strategic shift with an embodied ritualized movement that has gestural echoes of Dolores's "sign of the cross" blessing motion. Mario moves his fist skyward, heavenward, to bless collective resistance against neoliberal farm owner's death-dealing policies. Mario's signifying fist-as-blessing is a liberatory evolutionary step from his prior need to seek a blessing from his mother. Mario transitions from beseeching a blessing of his mother to conferring a blessing to his community—an extraordinary, agentic liberatory evolution.

Strategically, Mario shifts from rejecting bare life by escaping the neoliberal sovereign to rejecting bare life by confronting the neoliberal sovereign. Evidence of this strategic shift is found in the words that accompany his raised fist blessing: "Burn the fields!" During the play's climax, in a powerful reversal, Mario switches from seeking liberation by running from the McLaughlin fields to seeking liberation by running into the McLaughlin fields—to burn them. Mario directly engages the neoliberal sovereign by dealing death to the cash crops that motivated the neoliberal sovereign's death-dealing policies. Echoing *The Salt Eaters*'s Velma Henry's embodied answer to "Are you sure, sweetheart, that you want to be well?" Mario's moving body answers "yes" to wellness and "yes" to elevated animacy by answering "no" to bare life.

3

Animating Anthologies and Firing the Canon in *This Bridge Called My Back* and *June Jordan's Poetry for the People*

> We have got to know each other better and teach each other our ways, our views, if we're to remove the scales.
>
> —Toni Cade Bambara[1]

Different Sisters

In chapter 2, the imbricated relationship between ankhing and counterpublics is explored as a generative way to resist sovereign-related hegemony directed at Brown and Black communities, by engendering environments where animacy can be nurtured. Chapter 3 argues for an expansive understanding of the counterpublic notion by averring that radical anthologies can exist as counterpublics themselves. The chapter explores how ankhing's embrace of alterity and an egalitarian ethos can assist liberation-minded writers who organize via anthologies to reimagine possibilities that elevate people of color animacy. Furthermore, the chapter explores the ways in which the canon (and exclusion from it) pushes women of color writers toward bare life.

Writing about the intersection of race and anthologies, Brent Hayes Edwards opines, "[An anthology] necessarily 'presumes some idea of difference' . . . and aims to present the specific contours of that difference, in a way that both articulates it—makes it speak—and marks it off."[2] For Edwards, the racialized anthology can frame difference as a generative entity. The anthology has the power to speak and mark difference as a thing of value. The contributors to the influential anthologies *June Jordan's Poetry for the People* and *This Bridge Called My Back* give voice to difference and mark it as beautiful.

In the preface of Cherríe Moraga and Gloria Anzaldúa's foundational *This Bridge Called My Back: Writings by Radical Women of Color*, Moraga recounts touchstones in her political evolution. Moraga mentions travelling to African American writer/activist Barbara Smith's home to discuss the yet-to-be-completed *This Bridge* anthology and the lesbian-led, anti-racism organizing in Boston. Moraga writes:

> Barbara comes into the front room where she has made a bed for me. She kisses me. Then grabbing my shoulders, she says, very solid-like, 'We're sisters.' I nod, put myself into bed, and roll around with this word, *sisters*, for two hours before sleep takes on. I earned this with Barbara. It is not a given between us—Chicana and Black—to come to see each other as sisters. This is not a given. I keep wanting to repeat over and over and over again, the pain and shock of difference, the shock of commonness, the exhilaration of meeting through incredible odds against it.[3]

The above passage suggests that even as Moraga luxuriates in the burgeoning intercultural sisterhood rooted in emancipatory labor, "the shock of difference" reminds her of the challenges and opportunities that alterity brings. "Shocking" is a significant nomenclature choice as a difference descriptor. The *Oxford English Dictionary* defines the root word "shock" as, "A sudden or disturbing impression on the mind or feeling; usually, one produced by some unwelcome occurrence or perception, by pain, grief, or violent emotion."[4] In her meeting with a fellow queer writer and activist, who is African American, the word "sisters" leaves a disturbing impression (powerful enough to keep her tossing and turning for two hours) because Moraga is shocked by the tangible differences that race represents.

Moraga has much in common with Smith, a sisterly-like parallelism, so confronting their racial differences triggers the violent emotions and sleeplessness. During her tossing and turning, Moraga wants to keep repeating "sisters" over and over because she has to convince herself that sisterhood born of liberatory theory and praxis can overcome difference born of social construction and subject position. Race is socially constructed but its impact on some racialized subjects is so tangible that race concretizes difference. Race is real.

Although Moraga is challenged by the differences between Smith and herself, alterity is not demonized. Racial difference operates as a different type of opportunity: a difficult opportunity. Kohn argues that difference is a valued quality in heterotopias of resistance, because alterity creates opportunities for new epistemologies, which can lead to new liberatory best practices. In contradistinction, the dubious "color-blind" discourse popularized by conservative critic Shelby Steele's *The Content of Our Character* argues that race has an unnecessarily outsized role in society. Steele avers that racial animus will dissipate by ignoring racial difference, focusing on "character content" and by embracing a color-blind approach during sociopolitical interactions.[5] The color-blind approach is built on denying white supremacy's historical role in establishing American power and built on denying American structural racism's continuing deleterious impact on people of color.

Cohering with Kohn's embrace of alterity and rejecting Steele's imaginary erasure of difference, Moraga wrestles with difference, because she believes the emancipatory payoff will be profitable. Moraga frames her precarious sisterhood with Smith in the language of labor and payoff: "I earned this with Barbara." Moraga's earned sisterhood is emblematic of what heterotopias of resistance demand for effective emancipatory labor. However, interracial labor's precarious nature should not completely overshadow emancipatory labor's excitement. In the immediate aftermath of difference's disturbing impression, Moraga addresses the exultation of interracial liberatory labor: "the exhilaration of meeting through incredible odds against it."

Interestingly, the odds against effective multiracial, sociopolitical, and economic organizing enhances the excitement around this liberatory enterprise. The American neoliberal context often involves the most vulnerable competing for the fewest resources. As a result, creating Black and Brown environments that can be utilized to organize against hegemony function as an inspiring victory over neoliberal atomizing concerns. Moraga's struggle and embrace of shocking difference echoes an important stage in the ankhing process. In sociopolitical organizing driven by strategy and inspiration, the ankhing process privileges alterity, diverse ideas, democratic decision-making, and concomitant communal labor to implement democratically agreed upon courses of action. The ankhing process works well within heterotopias of resistance; both share a similar alterity-friendly, democratic ethos. As a multiracial, liberation-oriented anthology, *This Bridge Called My Back* functions as an artistic heterotopia of resistance because it is an alterity-friendly, democratic space and it is a space constructed and propelled by literary artists.

Bridge to Resistance

This Bridge Called My Back is a counterpublic space qua artistic heterotopia of resistance: it is "a real countersite that inverts and contests existing economic or social hierarchies. Its function is social transformation rather than escapism, containment, or denial. By challenging conventions of the dominant society, it can be an important locus of struggle against normalization."[6] This liberatory anthology is an artistic space inhabited by self-identified radical women of color who are interested (like Kohn) in "sites that foster oppositional practices by sheltering counterhegemonic ideas and identities."[7] Similarly, Maylei Blackwell argues that Chicana feminist print communities like *Hijas de Cuauhtémoc* and print communities that included Chicana feminist writings like *This Bridge Called My Back* constituted counterpublics in which, "print culture functioned as a mediating space where new ideas theories, and political claims were constructed, negotiated and contested."[8]

This Bridge Called My Back's forty-five writings[9] include a manifesto, poems, essays, commentary, letters, and interviews by Black, Latina, Asian, and Native American writers who, Angela Y. Davis argues, dispel "all doubt about the power of a single text to radically transform the terrain of our theory and practice. *This Bridge* has allowed us to define the promise of research on race, gender, class, and sexuality as profoundly linked to collaboration and coalition-building. And perhaps most important, it has offered us strategies for transformative political practice."[10] The first half of Davis's note hints at *This Bridge*'s role as an actant: a source of action that can be either human or nonhuman; it is that which has efficacy, can do things, has sufficient coherence to make a difference, produce effects, alter the course of events.[11] Davis writes that what *This Bridge* "can do" is "transform the terrain of our theory and practice." The second half of Davis's note about *This Bridge* offering "strategies for transformative political practice" suggests that this single text is engaging in the transformative labor that is a hallmark of heterotopias of resistance.

Using Kohn's nomenclature, *This Bridge*'s origin is rooted in a need for American feminist women of color to create "safe havens."[12] In the volume's Introduction, Moraga and Anzaldúa recount Anzaldúa's mistreatment by White feminists at a San Francisco-area women's retreat in February 1979 and the duo's experience with elitism and racism during a two-year stint working as the only two Chicanas for a national feminist writers organization.[13] Frustrated with the resistance to change, Moraga and Anzaldúa endeavor to create a safe haven for radical feminists of color. Their safe haven would not be another organization or an edifice. The editors explain that after the national feminist organization "repeatedly refused to address itself to its elitist and racist practices, we left the organization and began work on this book."[14] The writer-activists seek safety in a book. Structurally, *This Bridge* is an alternative public that consists of enough space to give each writer a "room of her own." The radical anthology structure is built on identity and difference.

In the original call for submission that would eventually lead to work accepted into *This Bridge*, Moraga and Anzaldúa write "we want to examine the incidents of intolerance, prejudice and denial of differences within the feminist movement. We intend to explore the causes and sources of, and solutions to these divisions. We want to create a definition that expands what 'feminist' means to us."[15] As a heterotopia of resistance, *This Bridge* provides a shelter for counter-hegemonic ideas and identities. The anthology provides a sheltered space for radical feminists of color to think through and work through their own understandings of feminist identities. Furthermore, *This Bridge* seeks to provide a safe haven where radical women of color can speak freely about intolerance and prejudice within a putatively liberatory feminist movement. While *This Bridge* is engaged in intrafeminist struggle, it does double-duty by simultaneously engaging in macro-level, liberatory labor: supporting equal rights, equitable treatment, and mutual respect for women in a national and international context often hostile towards women.

This intra-feminist and macro-level liberatory labor imbricates with the ankhing process, because in *This Bridge* radical feminists of color collectively think through the most effective means to resist hegemonic forces, and through this idea-exchange, inspire, motivate, and move each other toward best practices to resist hegemonic forces seeking to delimit their subjectivity, social, political, and economic agency, and delimit their power to determine their own life courses. Following Nancy Fraser, *This Bridge* coheres with the ankhing process by functioning as a subaltern counterpublic "where members of subordinated social groups invent and circulate counterdiscourses which in turn permit them to formulate oppositional interpretations of their identities, interests and needs."[16]

Of Poetry and Praxis

Similar to *This Bridge Called My Back*, June Jordan's *Poetry for the People: A Revolutionary Blueprint* serves as a space where counterdiscourses are circulated to formulate oppositional interpretations of identities, interests, and needs. In the pragmatic and powerful Introduction, June Jordan speaks about the alienation she experienced as a result of an American educational system that did not reflect her experiences or value her culturally-tethered epistemologies:

> When I was going to school, too much of the time I found myself an alien body force-fed stories and facts about people entirely unrelated to me, or my family . . . history or future. I was made to learn about 'the powerful': those who won wars or who conquered territory or whose odd ideas about poetry and love prevailed inside some distant country where neither of my parents nor myself would find welcome.[17]

The alien discourses foisted upon Jordan alienate her because they are not rooted in her cultural or experiential narratives. Instead, these "force-fed" stories are tied to sovereign narratives chronicling the use of sovereign power to win wars and conquer peoples. Jordan's educational experiences inspire her to create a heterotopia of resistance in the classroom. Jordan seeks to turn the university classroom into a real countersite that inverts and contests existing or social hierarchies.

Since Jordan views the imposition of "dead-White-men" literature curriculum as hegemonic, her resistance act is to radically reimagine what constitutes literatures worthy to be taught at an elite educational institution like the University of California Berkeley. Imbricated with Lipsitz's perspective, Jordan intends to teach works of expressive culture that "function as repositories of collective memory, sources of moral instruction, and mechanisms for transforming places and calling communities into being."[18] Finally dining on literature as a college student that represents her memory, history, and being, iconic Black feminist scholar Barbara Christian writes about the ontological health benefits that June Jordan's force-fed literature could not provide her:

> For me, *Brown Girl, Brownstones* was not just a text, it was an accurate and dynamic embodiment both of the possibilities and improbabilities of my own life. In it I as subject encountered myself as object. In illuminating so clearly, so lovingly, the mesh of my own context, [Paule] Marshall provided me with a guide, a way to contemplate my own situation and gave me back the memory, the embodied history of women like myself who had preceded me.[19]

By choosing to teach literature that centers women of color as subjects and objects who expand possibilities of embodied racialized matter, June Jordan expands university pedagogical possibilities. By aligning with heterotopias of resistance and decentering dead-White-men literature, June Jordan imagines a pedagogical space that challenges conventions of the dominant society and transforms the university classroom into a counterpublic that functions as an important locus of struggle against normalization. Decentering dead-White-men literature is a significant step against normalization; it necessitates centering diverse literatures and embracing difference itself. Decentering dead-White-men literature necessitates "rescuing the canon" by animating the canon: privileging aliveness over the dead.[20]

As an artistic counterpublic, *June Jordan's Poetry for the People* is vested in a collectivist approach to interrogating and reimagining the canon. However, before exploring this collectivist canon approach, it may be helpful to discuss the collectivist design of the book. *June Jordan's Poetry for the People* is a hyper-hybrid text. The book is an anthology in that it includes a collection of poems and essays about poetry from emergent student poets, including Ruth Forman and Samiya Bashir, and established literary figures, including Jordan, Adrienne Rich, Audre Lorde, Joy Harjo, and Ntozake Shange. The established and emerging poets are presented side-by-side. This non-hierarchical presentation privileges ideas and artistic merit over perceived status and name-recognition, while tacitly validating student poets' work.

Also, *Poetry for the People* is a pragmatic "blueprint" for how to develop a pedagogical and artistic counterpublic, including liberatory best practices that lead to the highest quality epistemological and artistic production. The book features specific writing techniques about how to speak individualized "truth" to sovereign power, approaches to workshop-oriented critique, sample syllabi, and sample reading lists from Asian American, Latinx, Caribbean, and African American Literatures, Children's Literatures, Women's Literatures, and Queer Literatures. Aligning with the ankhing process, and Kohn's argument regarding heterotopias of resistance, this embrace of alterity communicates a high valuation for difference as an effective technology in emancipatory cultural labor.

Poetry for the People highlights the importance of publishing and disseminating liberatory cultural labor in the form of poetry chapbooks and public readings at anti-war protests, political rallies, and State-controlled spaces like public universities. In her listing of counterpublic characteristics, Catherine Squires mentions:

> protest rhetoric; persuasion; increased interpublic communication and interaction with the state; occupation and reclamation of the dominant and state-controlled public space . . . foster resistance; test arguments and strategies in wider publics; create alliances; persuade outsiders to change views; perform public resistance to oppressive laws and social codes; gain allies.[21]

Like Squires, *Poetry for the People* focuses on the public presentation of liberatory cultural labor as a form of public protest rhetoric (against sovereign power) that seeks to foster resistance, persuade outsiders to change views, reclaim public space, create alliances, and gain allies. With great specificity, *Poetry for the People* lays out strategic ways to select work for publication, raise money, seek sponsorship, work with printers, organize public readings, effectively engage the media, and how to solicit critical feedback during these processes, so that as best practices are identified, they can consistently evolve and improve.

Poetry for the People's authorship signals its embrace of a democratic, non-hierarchical ethos. Although Poetry for the People's pedagogical approach is June Jordan's concept, and is included in *June Jordan's Poetry for the People*, she is not the author of the text—nor an editor. The text's editors are Lauren Muller and the Blueprint Collective. At the time of publication, Muller was a graduate student in the University of California Berkeley's English department where she had taught with Jordan for four years. The Blueprint Collective consists of Poetry for the People student poets (at the time of publication) Shanti Bright, Gary Chandler, Ananda Esteva, Sean Lewis, Stephanie Rose, Shelly Smith, Shelly Teves, Rubén Antonio Villalobos, and Pamela Wilson. The book was co-written in Muller's house, where "Four poets wrote quietly and intently in the bedroom; in the study and in the kitchen, there were five computers and facing each screen were two or three poets negotiating word choice, examples to prove a point, and paragraph placement."[22] June Jordan's communal approach to teaching the Poetry for the People class inspired the communal approach to writing *June Jordan's Poetry for the People*. Both of these communal processes imbricate with the communal labor ethos ankhing champions.

June Jordan's Poetry for the People's communal ethos informs how this artistic heterotopia of resistance addresses rescuing the canon—and from whom the canon needs to be rescued—and why there needs to be a rescue. The book includes analysis from established literary figures and student poets about the canon and its impact on their own lives and on American society in general. As Jordan suggests, when American subjects study canonized literature that does not reflect their experience, their experience is delegitimized. This delegitimization can result in feelings of soul-crushing alienation from the homeland, from the national public. As one consequence of the phenomena, subjects develop heterotopias of resistance to counter this death-dealing alienation.

Firing the Canon

In the counterpublic *June Jordan's Poetry for the People*, Adrienne Rich comments on encountering canonical poetry while writing poetry from the subject position of a relatively privileged young White woman (she was a student at Harvard during the period in question). This insightful passage is significant enough to quote at length:

> When the ideas or forms we need are banished, we seek their residues wherever we can trace them. But there was one major problem with this. I had been born a woman and I was trying to think and act as if poetry—and the possibility of making poetry—were a universal—a gender neutral. In the universe of masculine paradigm, I naturally absorbed ideas about women, sexuality, power from the subjectivity of male poets—Yeats not the least among them. The dissonance between these images and the daily events of my own life demanded a constant footwork of imagination, a kind of perpetual translation, and an unconscious fragmentation of identity: woman from poet. Every group that lives under the naming and image-making power of a dominant culture is at risk from this mental fragmentation and needs an art which can resist it.[23]

In discussing the "canonical voice" and its gendered representative, Rich conflates "universal" and "universe of masculine" to construct a literary sovereign. This masculine-gendered sovereign power has the power to communicate the sovereign experience as *experience itself*: the White male literary voice is the universal voice, the human voice. In its hyper-universality, the White male canonical voice doesn't have to proclaim its universality. Instead, as an embodiment of White male sociopolitical sovereign power, the White male canonical voice is universal, because the sovereign power insists that it is so. This insistence is produced in silence because that is the nature of sovereign power: sovereign power *is*.

When the "is-ness" of sovereign power is tethered to White male subjects, the "naturalness" of this sovereign power is extended to White male subjects. In the canon, the writings of talented White male writers become naturally universal. These writings are not seen as the specific expressions of White male subjectivity; they are seen as universal expressions of the human experience: universal expressions of aliveness. This state of affairs sets the stage for sovereign creative death-dealing through a canonical prism. As Rich experiences, in a masculine paradigm, non-White, non-male poets "naturally absor[b] ideas about women, sexuality, power from the subjectivity of male poets." Absorbing a powerful sovereign into a subject can have the effect of alienating the subject from herself or, as Rich describes the process, result in a "fragmentation of identity." The canon has the power to separate the self from the self. Fragmentation of identity is death-dealing by another name.

The canon's adverse impact on a relatively privileged White female subject suggests that the impact could be more adverse on subjects when class and race are introduced. The multiplier effect of interlocking oppressions (i.e., gender, class, race, sexuality oppressions) is difficult to quantify, but it is important to interrogate the ways in which these multiple oppressions impact women of color in relation to the canon. Poet Marilyn Chin writes, "It's a fixed endgame: There will always be an imperialist, Eurocentric bias. The powers-that-be who lord over the selection process are and forevermore will be privileged White male critics . . . What I learned from my youth as a marginalized and isolated west coast Asian American poet is this: it's no fun to be 'excluded' . . . as a matter of fact, it feels like hell."[24]

It is important to note that Chin uses the idiomatic expression "feels like hell" to articulate her experience of canonical exclusion.[25] In the American imaginary, hell functions as a teleological destination tethered to death and repetitive dying (see the related idiomatic expression "a living hell"). Chin is tying canonical exclusion to bare life for embodied racialized female subjects. Talented and deserving female writers of color become a kind of "walking dead/writing dead" vis-à-vis the canon. At times, these writers produce exceptional and acclaimed work (i.e., Chin), but the work itself exists on the outer boundaries of the living word.

The survival of women of color in the literary afterlife (which canonization provides) is curtailed because of exclusion from legacy-making anthologies that validate writers. Chin argues that this literary bare life for female writers of color is exacerbated by overwhelmingly White male critics who "will decide who will be validated along with Shakespeare and Milton and latter-day saints of the like of Keats, Yeats and Eliot. They will guard the 'canon' jealously with their elaborate 'critical' apparatus; and driven by their own Darwinian instinct to 'survive,' they will do the best they can to 'exclude' us."[26] Chin avers that White male critics have set up a zero-sum game of literary survival where the imbricated critical, scholarly, and publishing infrastructures favor White male writers. This favorable terrain for White male writers contributes to a literary environment where the White male's specific concerns, interests, desires, aspirations, fears, cosmologies, and aesthetic sensibilities become "universal" concerns, interests, desires, aspirations, fears, cosmologies, and aesthetic sensibilities. As a result, talented and ambitious female writers of color find themselves in a deadly trickbag: In order to write transcendent "universal" literature (and avoid literary hell), they must die to themselves, subvert authentic impulses, and write in a way that could be considered White male-identified.

Since many talented and ambitious women of color writers first get on the literary road to hell by learning about the canon through their educational processes, let us return to June Jordan's educational experience. Jordan confesses that she hated school, because the literature she was exposed to did not reflect her experience. Jordan was caught up in pedagogical and epistemological phenomena that could be entitled "Reading Dead White Men While Black." Jordan frames these dead White men as educational and artistic death-dealers: dead White male authors were killing Jordan. Jordan tethers dead White men literature to present historical moment oppression; she avers that this oppression can be overcome by educational and artistic alterity. Jordan argues that resisting death-dealing by the dead is emancipatory labor that has the power to liberate the self and subaltern communities from educational and artistic alienation. Commenting on the process of transforming the university space into a counterpublic, Jordan writes about overcoming the dead, "As a teacher I was learning how not to hate school: how to overcome the fixed, predetermined, graveyard nature of so much formal education: come and be buried here among these other (allegedly) honorable dead."[27]

Heterotopias of resistance can function as alternative educational spaces; they are democratic-oriented, pedagogical institutions where subjects teach each other to interrogate and acquire new epistemologies. *June Jordan's Poetry for the People* falls within this counterpublic sphere. The hybrid anthology is framed as (and subtitled) "a revolutionary blueprint." An architectural blueprint lays out the course of action to build a structure. This revolutionary blueprint lays out the course of action to build an art-based, pedagogical heterotopia of resistance.

Liberation Pedagogy

Brazilian pedagogical theorist Paulo Freire argues that education can be transformative for subaltern subjects when they are encouraged to transform themselves and their environments. Freire roots this transformative pedagogical process in his *conscientização* notion. *Conscientização* refers to "learning to perceive social, political, and economic contradictions, and to take action against the oppressive elements of reality."[28] Talented American women writers of color face the contradiction inherent in a canon that purports to represent the best literature in the English language, while seemingly basing its selection criteria on the best literature written by White males—and those who can effectively imitate White males' specific concerns, interests, desires, aspirations, fears, cosmologies, and aesthetic sensibilities.

Writers of color are often first exposed to the aforementioned contradictions in pedagogical institutions. In response to these artistic and pedagogical contradictions, *June Jordan's Poetry for the People*, as an artistic heterotopia of resistance, takes a pedagogical approach to resistance. The blueprint is designed to teach interested parties how to create and develop artistic counterpublics in their respective communities. However, the anthology's pedagogical approach to this revolutionary labor is not top-down. Instead, *June Jordan's Poetry for the People* embraces a democratic model featuring shared leadership, fluidity of teacher/student roles, the humanizing power of self-knowledge, and the import of liberatory praxis.

Jordan defines poetry as "A medium for telling the truth."[29] Jordan seems to embrace the indigenous Malian notion "nommo" (animating power of the spoken word) as a model for her understanding of word power. Words qua poetry have the power to affect and effect phenomena. The word can influence the body by moving it into action and influence the body politic by calling it into self-reflection. For Jordan, the word is a freedom agent: agency is its calling card. Freire's understanding of the word is imbricated with Jordan's understanding. Freire writes, "Within the word we find two dimensions, reflection and action, in such radical interaction, that if one is sacrificed—even in part—the other immediately suffers. There is no true word that is not at the same time a praxis. Thus to speak a true word is to transform the word."[30] Freire sees a dialectical relationship between word by-products (reflection and action), whereby reflection and action are informed and changed by each other. For interlocutors of the "true word," reflection and praxis alternatively teach and learn from one another as if they were subjects themselves. The two notions are engaged in a radical, dialectical interaction that animates both enough to bring more expansive life to the interlocutor.

For Jordan, the interlocutor is the poet who speaks the true word, and poetry is a medium for telling the truth. When this truth is spoken to manifestations of power, true word has the power to galvanize people in the direction of liberation. The galvanizing element is driven by poetry's ability to connect people to one another as they name sovereign silence. This naming can engender courage in the dispossessed and encourage them to name their individual and collective worlds. *June Jordan's Poetry for the People*'s editors assert that, "Poetry names what has been silenced and allows us to understand and articulate connections to one another and to the world we inhabit."[31] Freire approaches this intersection of true word, naming, and liberatory praxis in the following way:

> Human existence cannot be silent, nor can it be nourished by false words, but only with true words, with which men and women transform the world. To exist, humanly, is to *name* the world, to change it. Once named, the world in its turn reappears to namers as a problem and requires of them a new *naming*. Human beings are not built in silence, but in word, in work, in action-reflection.[32]

As a pedagogical technology, *June Jordan's Poetry for the People* is a revolutionary blueprint for creating artistic heterotopias of resistance, where subjects can name themselves and their respective communities.

Naming the self and the "collective we" is a subaltern power move. In Mel Y. Chen's analysis of the animacy hierarchy, those at the top of the hierarchy have the power to define and name those below them. In the United States context, socioeconomically and politically well-resourced White males (as top-dwellers) have the power to define and name (often with damaging names) people of color. Mel Y. Chen argues that, "Insults, shaming language, slurs and injurious speech can be thought of as tools of objectification, but these also, in crucial ways, paradoxically rely on animacy as they objectify, thereby providing possibilities for reanimation."³³ Objectification de-animates human subjects, effectively sliding them down the animacy hierarchy. This slippery slide is a death slide for racialized matter. Given the intersection of race and class oppression, these dual forces push people of color down into the nether regions of the human animacy scale, where bare life is a way of life. However, when subaltern subjects use true word to name the self, the process operates as a reanimating form of resistance. *June Jordan's Poetry for the People*, using poetry as true word, teaches subjects to build artistic counterpublics that can foment resistance against a neoliberal sovereign's atomizing gaze.

The aforementioned teaching aspect is critical to artistic counterpublic viability. In heterotopias of resistance, learning is often accompanied by unlearning. Subaltern subjects may need to unlearn the names (and their negative externalities) that were handed down from subjects higher on the animacy scale. This unlearning, this releasing of counterproductive epistemologies, makes room for new emancipatory knowledges to take root. Jordan and Freire argue that democratically-oriented, critical modes of dialogue are especially effective in the liberatory pedagogical process. Freire writes that, "Dialogue is the encounter between [men and women], mediated by the world, in order to name the world . . . If it is in speaking their word that people, by naming the world, transform it, dialogue imposes itself as the way by which they achieve significance as human beings."³⁴ In a pedagogical context, dialogue suggests respect between the interlocutors; it connotes mutuality in the learning process, whereby teacher and student are learning together, while creating new epistemologies from their dialectical engagement. This process stands in direct opposition to what Freire defines as the "banking" pedagogical approach.

The banking pedagogical approach is a top-down, unidirectional educational model. The teacher "deposits" information into a docile student. Freire writes:

> Education thus becomes an act of depositing, in which the students are depositories and the teacher is the depositor. Instead of communicating, the teacher issues communiqués and makes deposits which the students patiently receive, memorize and repeat. This is the "banking" concept of education, in which the scope of action allowed to the students extends only as far as receiving, filing, and storing

deposits . . . it is the people themselves who are filed away through the lack of creativity, transformation, and knowledge in this (at best) misguided system. For apart from inquiry, apart from the praxis, individuals cannot be truly human.[35]

Like Freire, Jordan is advocating for an educational model that rejects the student as a passive object. Instead, Jordan's model is rooted in creativity and freedom, and encourages the students to expand their subjectivity by critically, creatively, and freely exploring their human experience, and the human experience of others. "Creative-free-thinking" students situate their own personal experience, while exploring the human condition. In this broad human context, students are able to connect their life to the expressions of life around them, and thereby connect their life to human expressions of beauty, value, and power on the planet. Equally important, the creative-free-thinking student is more inclined to appreciate his or her own unique human expression as an essential contribution to humanity's diverse articulations of beauty, value, and power. This embrace of the human is not only tantamount to resisting objectification, it is tantamount to resisting the push toward animality.

Shaming-Naming

In *Animacies: Biopolitics, Racial Mattering and Queer Affect*, Chen close-reads an encounter where a sovereign representative uses insults and slurs ("shaming-naming") to push a subaltern subject toward animality in public. The public aspect of shaming-naming[36] creates a spectacle that validates and concretizes the dehumanization by allowing witnesses to "co-sign" the injurious behavior through their inability or unwillingness to stop the injurious behavior. At a public campaign rally related to his reelection in Virginia, United States Republican Senator George Allen was being video recorded by a volunteer from the opposing Democratic campaign of James Webb. The videographer was a Virginian of South Asian heritage named Shekar Ramanuja Sidarth who was ostensibly the only non-White person at the event.[37] Allen points to Sidarth and, unlike Jordan's use of "the word," publicly directs injurious words toward Sidarth in front of the all-White crowd:

This fellow here, over here with the yellow shirt, macaca, or whatever his name is. He's with my opponent. He's following us around everywhere and it's just great. . . . Let's give a welcome to macaca, here. Welcome to America and the real world of Virginia.[38]

Macaca is Tunisian slang for monkey and the term is used as a racial pejorative toward darker-skinned Tunisians who are referred to as "Blacks."[39] Although Chen concurs with journalists who raised concerns about the sociopolitical problematics of a White sovereign representative comparing a dark-skinned subaltern subject to a monkey, she troubles the notion of the a priori hierarchical relationship between humans and simians.[40]

The horizontal relationship elements that may exist between human beings and monkeys not withstanding, Allen's public comparison between dark-skinned Sidarth and a simian was meant as a public slur. Allen was attempting to dehumanize the only person of color at a political gathering, by not only hailing him as a simian, but by suggesting that his arrival at the all-White United States senatorial event was Sidarth's introduction "to America and the real world of Virginia." Allen insinuates that Virginian resident and American citizen Sidarth is legitimately neither Virginian resident nor American citizen because his dark skin drops him down the animacy hierarchy (from Allen's perspective) to the "no-man's land" between animality and bare life.

The illegitimating aspect of Allen's shaming-naming encounter with Sidarth aligns with the troubling American tradition of top animacy scale dwellers calling into question the legitimate citizenship of relatively lower animacy scale dwellers. While acknowledging historical and contemporary anti-Blackness (and its effects and affects), this study argues that African Americans, in particular, should claim the benefits that purportedly accrue to American citizens, because a substantial amount of sociopolitical and economic prosperity (i.e., during slavery) has been built on the exploitation of Black labor and Black cultural production. It is possible to embrace these citizen-tethered benefits *and* offer cogent critiques of State-sponsored violence, the prison industrial complex, environmental racism, and other forms of institutionalized violence.

In this present historical moment of heightened xenophobia, American citizens who are not European American are increasingly vulnerable to shaming-naming and other State-endorsed, sociopolitical technologies that deem their citizenship illegitimate. It may be helpful here to explore Lisa Lowe's understanding of how the State and its representatives engage darker citizens. In *Immigrant Acts: On Asian American Cultural Politics*, Lowe propels her study by arguing that Asian-American culture is an arena of contestation, a forum where Americans of Asian descent, and by extension, other ethnic Americans, can articulate a complex American subjectivity (versus the "homogenous" abstract citizen expression) that does not require them to forget a history of exclusion, racism, racialized violence and gendered oppression.[41]

Lowe's position differs from Marx's well-known assertion that capitalism maximizes profits by exploiting (homogenized) abstract citizen's abstract labor. In contradistinction, Lowe argues that it is through differentiation of the racialized subject that capitalism maximizes profits. Through juridical moves which seek to interpellate non-White citizens as other (and therefore less), the State's imposed exploitation-motivated alterity allows it to pay "the other" less, provide less service, and generally treat racialized subjects "less than" in an effort to protect profits in legally and *culturally* sanctioned ways.[42] As an outgrowth of this hegemonic process, many racialized subjects accept this treatment even though they are nominally American citizens. Lowe argues that her exploration of the Asian-American interaction with the State can inform an analysis of other marginalized peoples in relation to the State.

For Lowe, racialized bodies are marked as excess, and not "naturally" available for citizenship. When Senator Allen uses a "bad word" (macaca) and tells East Asian Virginian citizen Sidarth, "Welcome to America and the real world of Virginia," Allen uses Sidarth's East Asian racialized body to exclude him from the political gathering of citizens. Lowe argues that through legal, juridical, and cultural means, racialized bodies are excluded from citizenship through a series of exclusion acts based on their bodies' racialized forms.[43] However, there is a way for the racialized subject to become a "naturalized" citizen. If they are willing forget their past and let go of memory, a deal can be struck. Racialized subjects can be liberated from their racialized skin by embracing fiction that doesn't necessarily live on a page. Lowe writes:

> [F]or Asians within the history of the United States—as for African Americans, Native Americans or Chicanos—'political emancipation' through citizenship is never an operation confined to the negation of individual 'private' particulars . . . [Accepting abstract citizenship] requires acceding to a political fiction of equal rights that is generated through the denial of history, a denial that reproduces the omission of history as the ontology of the nation.[44]

Sidarth is unwilling to accede to the political fiction of equal rights, evidenced by his volunteer work documenting the racist and xenophobic attitudes of a sitting member of the United State Senate. Furthermore, Sidarth's "fiction refusal" is seen in his written response to the perceived animacy scale positioning of South Asian citizens in America: "I am macaca."[45]

On June 16, 2015, in New York City's Trump Towers, Donald Trump announced his candidacy for President of the United States. Trump's announcement speech was defined by what Chen would call "insults, shaming language, slurs and injurious speech." Donald Trump's words are in direct opposition to Jordan's nommo-tethered use of the word and in direct opposition to Freire's "true words with which men and women transform the world." While discussing Mexican nationals who are interested in coming to the United States, Trump said:

> When Mexico sends its people, they're not sending their best. They're not sending you. They're not sending you. They're sending people that have lots of problems and they're bringing those problems with us. They're bringing drugs, they're bringing crime, they're rapists, and some, I assume, are good people.[46]

The association that Trump draws between Mexican immigrants and base criminality is made the more troubling, because these words were uttered during a presidential candidacy announcement speech. A man vying for a multi-ethnic country's highest office starts his campaign by shaming-naming an entire ethnic group. One can argue Trump's slur-strategy was propelled by his belief that verbally pushing Mexican nationals (and many Latinx folk by association) toward bare life was "good politics" because he was eventually elected president of the United States. Like Allen, Trump seemed to be staking his campaign on exciting a critical mass of primarily European-American voters and organizing them around the idea that they were the "real Americans." In Trumpian political logic, as real Americans, these European-American citizens would be able to elevate themselves sociopolitically by defining themselves higher on the human animacy scale vis-à-vis racialized subjects. The message to racialized Mexican citizens seems to be "you are not like real Americans; you are like those rapists and murderers across the border."

The irony of Trump's troubling message is that parts of present-day border states New Mexico, California, and Texas were forcibly taken April 1846 to February 1848, during what the Mexican government refers to as the Invasión estadounidense a México (United States' Invasion of Mexico). Article IX of the resultant Treaty of Guadalupe Hidalgo granted American citizenship with full civil rights to Mexican nationals who chose to stay within the new treaty-defined United States borders.[47] As Richard Griswold del Castillo makes clear and Lisa Lowe echoes, in order for the treaty-minted Mexican-American citizens to believe in the civil rights guarantees inherent in American citizenship, their belief required them to accede "to a political fiction of equal rights."

Against the History of Forgetting

Soon after the Treaty of Guadalupe Hidalgo was signed, the issue of equal rights guarantees was on the mind of newly designated Mexican-American powerbrokers. In 1849, during California's constitutional convention, six of the delegates were Native Californians (former Mexican citizens). These Mexican-American delegates were concerned that new Mexican-Americans whose phenotypes resembled Native Americans would face discrimination, including not being able to exercise the franchise.[48] The perceived animacy scale positioning of the indigenous Native Indian population and the new Mexican-Americans would influence a critical delegate decision regarding the intersection of race and rights. Griswold del Castillo suggests that although the Mexican-American delegates were aware of the racism driving the decision-making logic of the Anglo delegates, the Brown delegates ultimately voted:

> for the protection of their class even if it meant endorsing the racist views of their Anglo colleagues towards Indians and Blacks. Mexico had granted citizenship to 'civilized' Indians and to Blacks, and the Treaty of Guadalupe Hidalgo clearly stated that former Mexican citizens would be given the opportunity to become citizens of the United States. Following the biases of their age, the framers of the state constitution sought wording that would exclude Blacks and Indians while including Mexicans . . . It extended the vote to 'every White, male citizen of Mexico who shall have elected to become a citizen of the United States.'[49]

Presidential candidate Trump's aggressive xenophobic demonization of Mexican immigrants and Mexican-American citizens is further entrenched in irony, because some of the people he is demonizing come from families whose citizenship predates Trump's German immigrant grandfather Friederich Trump, who became a citizen in 1892.[50] The "insults, shaming language, slurs and injurious speech" allows sovereign power representatives like Trump to usher Brown bodies toward bare life—a move which helps create a sociopolitical environment, whereby injurious speech can lead to injured Brown bodies. Words matter.

Following Freire and Lowe, "true words" matter, because they are a resistance strategy against forgetting and omission; true words are a technology to name the "political fiction of equal rights that is generated through the denial of history, a denial that reproduces the omission of history as the ontology of the nation." *This Bridge Called My Back* and *June Jordan's Poetry for the People* are true word anthologies against forgetting. Referencing the American tradition of wearing ribbons to remember and support American military troops, Moraga counters with, "If we must wear ribbons, let us tie them around our finger to remind us of the daily practice of countering US collective amnesia . . . We must insist on what we remember to be true."[51] True word is often tied to memory so culturally-tethered memories can be a resistance resource. In *This Bridge Called My Back*, Max Wolf Valerio taps into her Native American (and Mexican ancestral) cultural history as a liberatory technology. In the context of battling both external material oppression against the Indian Nation and fighting a legacy of internalized hieroglyphics of the flesh, Valerio's resistance strategy is the following: "I remember the place where the sun does not malign the seasons flutes of penitents & headdressess for the Okan we rub our offerings of dried meat into the earth and the holy woman comes out and dances she is wearing the sacred headdress."[52] Together Moraga and Valerio are suggesting a salvific role for memory. Both writers make sacred the process of knowing the self by remembering the past. As an inversion of socioreligious hegemony, both writers are arguing that their community members may be healed by immersing themselves in the baptismal of cultural memory.

4

Wanda Coleman and Kamau Daáood Sing the Blues for the Black Body

Uniting the scars to make something beautiful the healer speaks.[1]

—Kamau Daáood

Love and the Gospel of Hate

Chapter 3 argues for an expansive understanding of the counterpublic notion, while averring that radical anthologies can exist as counterpublics themselves. The chapter also explores how ankhing's embrace of an egalitarian ethos and alterity can assist culturally-tethered, activist writers who gather in anthologies to reimagine possibilities that elevate the animacy of people of color. Furthermore, chapter 3 explores how the canon can push women of color writers toward bare life. Chapter 4 argues that the often surreal nature of American Black life (which often pushes Black folk toward bare life) calls for a surrealist approach to art that is rooted in creative freedom. The chapter argues that ankhing's liberatory embrace of art and Spirit engenders artistic freedom. The chapter also explores how this artistic freedom directly enhances Black surrealists' animacy and the animacy of those who consume Black surrealist art.

It was a Wednesday night, so the regulars had come to hear a "true word."[2] The Black vernacular usage and Freire's usage of true word are rooted in the conflation of word and deed. The Bible Study story that Wednesday night was specifically about the word and included verses 4:16–17 from the Gospel of Mark. In this pedagogical passage, Jesus is presented as a master teacher who has gathered his closest students to share with them wisdom narratives called parables about a farmer who sows words:

> Others, like seed sown on rocky places, hear the word and at once receive it with joy. But since they have no root, they last only a short time. When trouble or persecution comes because of the word, they quickly fall away.[3]

At the end of Bible Study, the regulars closed their eyes in preparation for the traditional Black benediction, "May the Lord watch between me and thee when we are absent one from another."[4] The regulars never uttered this prayer because persecution had come and spoken first from the lone visitor's 45-caliber muzzle. Bible Study regular Felecia Sanders later recalled that behind her shut eyelids, the first shot "sounded like a transformer blew . . . he caught us with our eyes closed."[5]

Sanders opened her eyes to see 21-year-old Dylann Roof shoot her 26-year-old son Tywanza Sanders and her 87-year-old aunt Susie Jackson. During the elongated shooting, and screaming, and reloading, and running, and hiding, and praying, and reloading, and confusion, and blood, and Bibles, and chasing, and reloading, Felecia Sanders was able to effectively play dead. This stealth strategy couldn't shield her ears: "And I just heard—I heard every shot. I heard every single shot."[6] Although wounded several times and reduced to crawling, Tywanza Sanders tried to shield others with his Black body, including Aunt Susie. Felecia Sanders heard her son cry out, "Where's Aunt Susie? I've got to get to Aunt Susie."[7] Felecia Sanders, momentarily, opened her eyes and started watching her son crawl toward his great-aunt, "And he didn't stop until he got to Aunt Susie . . . He got there. He got there. I said 'I love you, Tywanza.' He said, 'Mama, I love you. I love you.' And I watched him take his last breath."[8] Then, Felecia Sanders closed her eyes too: she had to play dead to live.

Tywanza Sanders, Susie Jackson, and seven others died during The Charleston Massacre at historic Emanuel African Methodist Episcopal on June 17, 2015, in Charleston, South Carolina.[9] Hours before the murders, the shooter Dylann Roof posted a racist manifesto on the white supremacist website lastrhodesian.com which included:

Niggers are stupid and violent. At the same time, they have the capacity to be very slick . . . We have no skinheads, no real KKK [in Charleston], no one doing anything but talking on the internet. Well someone has to have the bravery to take it to the real world, and I guess that has to be me.[10]

Roof's unimaginable and unspeakable actions and manifesto bring to mind scholar Jerod Sexton's efforts to make sense of this present historical moment's anti-Blackness. Responding from his subject position as a citizen, an African American, and a scholar, Sexton appears to struggle to express his concerns:

You think also, in this moment, about the unspeakable, perhaps unimaginable ways that black lives have been devalued, and you have trouble determining when to start the story—or history or mythology or fable—or how far afield to draw your sphere of concern.[11]

Roof's hate-filled, racist words stood in stark contrast to the words that victims' family members expressed to Roof, and the nation, at the killer's televised bond hearing two days after the massacre. Amidst extraordinary grief, the mourners told Roof that they forgave him and that love would win, not hate. After Felecia Sanders said, "We welcomed you Wednesday night in our Bible Study with open arms," Daniel Simmons, Sr.'s granddaughter, Alana Simmons somehow found a sliver of beauty in this latest blues chapter of Black peoples' story in America, and spoke a true word to domestic terrorist Dylann Roof: "Although my grandfather and the other victims died at the hands of hate, this is proof, everyone's plea for your soul is proof, that they—they lived in love and their legacies will live in love. So hate won't win."[12] Echoing Daáood's epigraph that starts this chapter, the massacre's mourners stitched their "scars to make something beautiful."

Army of Healers

Los Angeles-based poet Kamau Daáood's work interrogates the intersection of the beauty and blues in the Black community. Given the virulent anti-Blackness which has defined Black folks' sojourn in the United States, Daáood seems interested in understanding, documenting, and interpreting African Americans' capacity to create sublimity in the context of bare life. Kamau Daáood (along with fellow Los Angeles-based poet Wanda Coleman) functions as a blues poet qua community healer. Similar to *The Salt Eaters* community healer Minnie Ransom, Daáood draws from culturally-tethered, African-related traditions to engage in his urban curandero work. Minnie Ransom uses Black music as a liberatory healing modality while Daáood *centers* Black music as a liberatory healing technology. Daáood aligns with Cone when the scholar argues, "Black music is unity music. It unites the joy and the sorrow, the love and the hate, the hope and the despair of Black people; and it moves the people toward the direction of total liberation."[13] Daáood juxtaposes joy and sorrow, hope and despair, in ways that are often surprising and surreal. The poet's surrealist oeuvre has been informed by Los Angeles's surreal juxtaposition of ethnic diversity and ethnic segregation, extreme wealth and crushing poverty, and progressive racial politics and virulent anti-Blackness.[14] For Daáood, spatial and racial concerns shape poetic cultural production.

The poem "Army of Healers" is emblematic of Daáood's concerns and his approach to cultural labor. The five-part poem is a surreal urban elegy. In part one, "Army of Healers" starts broadly and lays out the crux of its multitudinous, poetic argument in the concise opening line: "Art is life."[15] "Art is life" is the natural extension of Lipsitz's Black spatial imaginary move, which asserts that Black cultural producers proceed from a "philosophy that sees art as a vital *part of life*." In contradistinction to the aforementioned emancipatory labor tradition of art being relegated to liberatory fringe, this opening line repositions art. Daáood's initial line not only centers art, it equates art with life, art with animacy. Consequently, Daáood animates art. In emancipatory movements, liberatory artists often have an ironic "fringe" existence (i.e., as warm-up acts, in-between speech filler, or closing performers). By arguing that art is life, Daáood resists the fringe for liberatory artists.

For Daáood, liberatory artists are human being producers of life, of heightened human animacy, so they must be central to human life—and, as a result, liberatory artists may have a heightened sense of knowledge about "what it means" to be human beings. Daáood's bold assertion (which teeters on romanticizing artists) echoes writer James Baldwin's position about artists:

> [The artist's struggle] must be considered as a metaphor for the struggle that is universal and daily for all human beings on the face of this terrifying globe to get to become human beings . . . the poets, by which I mean all artists, are the only people who know the truth about us.[16]

Aligning with Baldwin, Daáood doubles-down on his "art is life" opening line by averring in lines two through four: "[Art is] the raw material to sculpt joy / and meaning / religion and science in a mix."[17] Here, Daáood builds upon his claim that art is life, by also suggesting that art is a "meaning-making" technology which helps human beings make sense of art as life on this "terrifying globe." Art is "raw material," so art is matter: matter whose level of animacy is fluid according to Daáood. Daáood and Baldwin suggest that when art is placed in the service of meaning-making and epistemological acquisition, art can function as a mix of religion and science (both meaning-making technologies), and, when employed, this religion-science combination may elevate a subject's position on the human animacy scale.

Daáood's religio-scientific understanding of art is reminiscent of Matthew Arnold's perspective on art's religio-scientific potentialities:

> We should conceive of [art] as capable of higher uses, and called to higher destinies, than those which, in general, men have assigned to it hitherto. More and more mankind will discover that we have to turn to poetry to interpret life for us, to console us, to sustain us. Without poetry, our science will appear incomplete; and most of what now passes with us for religion and philosophy will be replaced by poetry. Science, I say, will appear incomplete without it.[18]

By identifying poetry's "higher destinies," Arnold is carving out a salvific role for poetry. Conflating Daáood's, Baldwin's, and Arnold's imbricated perspectives, the triumvirate collectively suggest that art is life and art can save a subject's life by resurrecting a subject's animacy from bare life. Specifically, in the first section of "Army of Healers," Daáood suggests that the poet, as healer, can heal herself. Daáood concludes the poem's first section with "this is an army of healers / physician heal thyself / and radiate, radiate."[19] By demonstrating, sharing, and radiating this "auto-salvific" energy, Daáood argues that poets can inspire other subjects to heal themselves as well.

The Surreal Stress Blues

In the third movement of "Army of Healers," Daáood begins to highlight the surrealist and music intersection with "the flowers have eyes / if they had mouths / their song would slay us."[20] Daáood's flower personification (ascribing sight to flowers) is a move that has a series of interrelated effects. As beauty objects, flowers have currency. In the transnational context, roses are cut from their native environment and are exchanged between subjects as symbols of love, appreciation, and condolence (at funerals). The United States's six-billion-dollar floral industry is a testament to aggressive, profit-driven nature objectification.[21] Amidst this profit-driven objectification, Daáood's flowers with eyes become witnesses. Following Carolyn Forché's "poetry of witness" notion (poetry that documents societal "situations of extremity"), "Army of Healers" functions as a poem of witness.[22]

For Daáood, flowers omnipresence in nature uniquely allows them to serve as witnesses to nature decimation (including their own profit-based uprooting) caused by human beings. These "domesticated" flowers become more powerful witnesses once they enter human living spaces. In particular, Daáood, poetically asserts that flowers are witnesses to societal "situations of extremity" involving the Black community. These flowers with eyes are positioned to watch the travails of Black bare life. The floral observers see and "know the chains on [Black folk's] tongues are rusty and blue / slow suicide that stretches over a life span."[23] This knowing is both Black knowledge and blues knowledge, blues epistemology, leveraged to explain the antebellum origins of Black suffering and resistance, which is coterminous with Clyde Woods assertion that "[t]he blues epistemology is a longstanding African American tradition of explaining reality and change. This form of explanation finds its origins in the processes of African American construction within, and resistance to, the antebellum plantation regime."[24] Daáood's chained tongue construction is a slavery image referencing the antebellum and postbellum reality of constricted verbal agency. Black subjects are not able to freely speak about Black bare life horrors, because sovereign power demands silent suffering from the oppressed. When the oppressed do "speak the unspeakable," the unavowable, when the oppressed do speak a true word to power, the sovereign delegitimizes their suffering and often marks bare life bodies similar to how *Heroes and Saints*'s Latinx community members' bodies are marked. This state of affairs gives insight into why the chains on the tongue are rusty and blue. Daáood suggests that being denied the ability to speak one's story is emotionally and physically painful. Literally, the denial of the ability to speak has the power to give one the emotional and physical blues. The poet argues that enforced silence damages the souls of Black folk and enforced silence contributes to the physical oppression that results from circumscribed agency. The chains are rusty because they are a legacy of slavery: these blues chains have caused the blues long enough for rust to form on the chains.

Black bare life's unspeakable horrors can be so debilitating ("slow suicide that stretches over a life span") that if the flower witnesses "had mouths / their song would slay us." Slay, here, is a reference to the performance-related vernacular term "kill," (as in, "she killed it"), which signifies powerfully affecting an audience. If these flower witnesses had mouths to testify in song about Black bare life, they could emotionally move listeners. These flowers could "kill" when singing about life that resembles slow suicide. Daáood does not gift flowers with mouths to sing a moving ode for those who suffer. However, the Black sufferers can sing their own song. For Daáood, Black speaking voices have been delimited by rusty chains, but Black music has found a way to break a link. Daáood avers that when speech fails to articulate the Black experience, blues people turn toward music to tell their bare life blues: they turn to art for their healing.

In section four, "Army of Healers" as a poem of witness testifies about a specific Black musician's life, "Arthur learned to finger the saxophone / by picking cotton with bloody fingers at the age of five."[25] In this situation of extremity, Daáood's "picking cotton" image is instructive. As a cash crop in the early nineteenth-century American agrarian South, the cotton industry was the Southern economy's financial engine—and, by extension, the American economy's financial engine as the nation's largest export in a web of global capitalism. Discussing the Mississippi Valley, the engine of the engine, historian Walter Johnson writes:

> [T]he daily standard of measure to which slaves in the Mississippi Valley were held marked the conceptual reach of the global economy in the first half of the nineteenth century: lashes into labor into bales into dollars into pounds sterling. Cotton planters, moreover, were not simply

> concerned with their slave-generated profits (although they surely were); they were concerned about their slaves' *productivity* . . . Between 1820 and 1860, the productivity of the average slave on the average cotton plantation in Mississippi increased sixfold.[26]

Daáood tethers the cotton-picking, saxophone-playing subject to the building of American productivity, the building of American wealth. This is a wealth that cannot be separated from the peculiar calculus of "lashes into labor into bales into dollars into pounds sterling." Johnson argues that Black bodies were pushed toward higher efficiency for immediate profits *and* as an insidious savings-and-loan entity: "Slaveholders stored their savings in slaves."[27] This financial arrangement is significant because it guaranteed that slaveholders were able to exploit Black present moments *and* exploit Black futures by monetizing the oppression saved "inside Black bodies." In this process, Black bodies became repositories for slaveholders' dreams. The cruel irony is that the individual slaveholder deposited his own dream (financial freedom) into the Black body, while squeezing out the slave's own dream (bodily freedom). This is the type of bare life existence that can silence the tongue with rusty chains. Can the subaltern speak—when the squeezed dream is silenced?

As Daáood's representative subaltern subject, Arthur breaks the silence with art. Arthur's saxophone articulates the precarious balancing act of Dreaming While Black. Arthur "moistens his [saxophone] reeds with dreams he collected / as he sang spirituals by his grandmother's knees."[28] The saxophone mouthpiece's vibrating reed (which produces the saxophone's sound) is usually made from giant cane (arundo donax), a plant used in some folk cultures for healing purposes (as a diuretic, as a treatment for malaria, etc.), and a plant which has religio-ritual functionality.[29] In ancient Egypt, arundo donax leaves were used in the ritualized wrapping of the dead. The ceremonial cane preserved Black bodies so they could tell their spiritual stories in the afterlife.[30] The ceremonial cane in Arthur's saxophone mouthpiece allows him to musically reinterpret the spirituals he sang "by his grandmother's knees." Arthur's grandmother is the conduit for the hieroglyphics of the flesh. The matriarch passed down her musical strategy, her salvific spirituals, for surviving oppression's ceremonial markings of the flesh and soul. Arthur's own spirituals first must make the middle passage across moist vibrating cane before his bare life song can exit the saxophone.

Following Fred Moten, Arthur's "shriek turns speech turns song"[31] as the song is crossing cane and "his soul spills out from the bell of his horn / sometimes he vomits flowers sometimes barbwire / it depends on what his heart had to stomach / the night before."[32] Daáood's nomenclature is significant here. Arthur's bare life blues "spills out" the saxophone. "Spills (as opposed to "blows" or "blasts") suggest the spilling of blood. Blood is the haunting complement to hieroglyphics of the flesh. Blood's haunting presence just below the marked racialized skin is the vehicle that, as Hortense Spillers argues, allows for the generational handing down of oppression from Black body to Black body: blood carries the phenotype of oppression's marker and memory. In the American historical context, the blood coursing just beneath Black skin has consistently surfaced as a result of virulent anti-Blackness. In America, Black bodies too often bleed. Bloodletting's soulful song is what spills out of Arthur's saxophone.

In "Army of Healers," there is a quick shift from blood that is forced from the body to another substance that is forced from the body:

> [S]ometimes he vomits flowers
> sometimes barbwire
> it depends on what his heart had to stomach
> the night before.[33]

Arthur's response to Black bare life is physical illness. This physical reaction to hieroglyphics of the flesh signifies the relationship between psycho-social oppression and the body. According to the Centers for Disease Control and Prevention, African-American hypertension rates are significantly higher than European-American rates and Black male hypertension-related mortality rates (often caused by heart attacks) are approximately double European-American male mortality rates. Furthermore, "Several studies found an association between racism and higher blood pressure levels in African American men. Perceived racism contributes to stress and low self-esteem, which can ultimately negatively affect blood pressure levels."[34] Arthur's psycho-social oppression experience makes him vomit flowers or barbwire depending "on what his heart had to stomach." Through verse, Daáood echoes the

CDC's findings regarding oppression's impact on the heart: racism breaks Black hearts—possibly unto death.

It is significant that Arthur's broken heart makes him vomit barbwire. Barbwire is a ubiquitous presence in the carceral industries. Jails, prisons, and other punitive detainment centers use barbwire to keep subjects from escaping their bare lives. Also, barbwire is a not-so-distant relative to slave chains which kept subjects from escaping their bare lives. This generational link between slave chains and barbwire is a signifier for the generational link between Black bare life during slavery and Black bare life in this present historical moment. The "chains on [Black] tongues are rusty," because they have been passed down from prior eras and these generational chains contribute to the present historical moment's propensity for detaining Black bodies behind barbed wire. Black bodies (marked with hieroglyphics of the flesh) are the literal connective tissue between slave chains and barbwire. Spillers argues that this generational substitution of slave chains for barbwire is what keeps Black subjects captive:

> These undecipherable markings on the captive body render a kind of hieroglyphics of the flesh whose severe disjunctures come to be hidden to the cultural seeing by skin color. We might well ask if this phenomenon of marking and branding actually 'transfers' from one generation to another, finding its various *symbolic substitutions* in an efficacy of meanings that repeat the initiating moments.[35]

This generational transfer of bare life captivity is made possible, because Black subjects have internalized chains and barbwire to such an extent that traces of chains and barbwire dwell in the blood. For many African Africans, oppression has set up residence beneath the epidermis. Some Black bodies are occupied territory. The barbwire-walls, with undecipherable markings, may be hidden inside, but the psycho-social illness they engender is powerful enough to make Arthur vomit barbwire.

It is important to note that Arthur vomits flowers from his saxophone as well. This bare life representative has the agency to transform internalized oppression into flowers, pain into beauty. Arthur is a bluesman. Arthur does what the blues requires: turn hardship into art. The flowers that emerge from Arthur's saxophone are liberatory. This musical beauty frees Arthur from completely being defined by oppression. As a bluesman, Arthur is more than the sum of his hardships; he is more than a victim. Arthur is a blues curandero. In transforming his pain into beauty, the bluesman exhales his story across the vibrating, healing cane as part of the self-healing process.

Arthur vomits barbwire, too, so flowers don't eliminate oppression; beauty doesn't make pain disappear. Yet, art can serve as a curative response to the illness that racism produces. For Daáood, Arthur is in an army of healers along with bare life Black artists who heal themselves. Daáood asserts, "This is an Army of Healers, / physician heal thyself / and radiate, radiate."[36] Daáood encourages healers to "radiate, radiate," because sharing medicinal energy can have a curative impact on the Black community. Arthur's self-healing process involving breath, medicinal arundo donax, and a saxophone has the power to radiate through an audience and play a curative role for those bare life listeners living with rusty chains on their tongues—and barbwire in their stomachs.

America Scars Its Young

"Arthur was born in America" is how Daáood starts the poem's fourth movement.[37] "Army of Healers" is an American poem. The poem's title is an ironic nod to America's consistently militarized approach to disciplining racialized bodies within the State and outside the State. America's policing apparatus has a troubling, well-documented, history of delimiting the freedom of racialized subjects—at times engaging in this circumscription in the name of American freedom. Daáood's "Army of Healers" functions as an embodied reminder about the false narrative regarding America as "the Land of the Free." The narrative history of America's Black racialized subjects is a story of chains and barbwire. The Black narrative includes a litany of blues songs in the language of saxophones. These minor key shrieks and screams are not found in America's "The Star Spangled Banner," but they are seen in "This Is America" (http://smarturl.it/TcigA), hip hop artist Donald Glover's 2018 music video qua visual critique of American violence on Black bodies. Daáood's Black shrieks and screams are the healing response to the bare life experience of African Americans living under the American flag.

In the poem's fifth and final section, Daáood turns to the future by turning toward Black youth. Initially, the fourth section situated Arthur at his grandmother's knees learning bare life survival strategies. The fifth section departs from Arthur's specific embodiment as a bare life representative and broadens to a macro discussion of unnamed Black youth. These children are unnamed but not unmarked. Daáood writes "urban tribal scars / decorate the cheeks of young scholars / endangered as those in tar pits."[38] These "urban tribal scars" are hieroglyphics of the flesh. These generational markings are already present on young Black bodies. Daáood signals that Black youth are haunted by the hand-me-down pain of their "impotent parents bleeding in the shadows."[39] These parents are impotent because they cannot protect their children from sovereign representatives who seek to push them down the animacy scale toward the same shadows where so many Black parents dwell: the shadows of bare life.

As marked candidates for the shadows of bare life, the margins of the American Dream, Black youth are "endangered as those in tar pits."[40] Like dinosaurs trapped in Los Angeles's La Brea Tar Pits, Black children face a death-dealing future. Not only are Black youth dealing with the same external and internal chains and barbwire that their parents are struggling against, numerous Black children are facing additional existential impediments. Daáood argues that African Americans are stuck in tar pits constitutive of "savage red streets,"[41] poorly performing school systems, food deserts, and an American policing apparatus that aggressively operates as if some Black lives don't matter.

Black children marked by hieroglyphics of the flesh, respond with "hieroglyphics sprayed on walls."[42] Daáood claims that Black youth, like their parents, turn to art to tell their blues stories. Young graffiti artists tell their bare life narratives on neoliberal State structures. This urban visual art complement to hip hop narratives provides marked youth an opportunity to mark the physical embodiments of the capitalist State. In America, where corporations have some legal protections which mirror legal protections for people, "Army of Healers" hints that corporate properties are protected more effectively than Black children.[43] In this context, young Black graffiti artists draw blues stories on American walls. Daáood avers that graffiti qua liberatory art signifies that Black youth are not defined by the oppressive walls around them—inclusive of walls with barbwire. Kamau Daáood ends "Army of Healers" with a poetic charge for Black children to look beyond a barbwire future—and inside themselves for healing: "This is an army of healers / physician heal thyself / and radiate, radiate."[44]

The Marking of Identity

Wanda Coleman, like Daáood, uses blues motifs to explore hieroglyphics of the flesh marking Black folk. In Coleman's dynamic and incisive poetry collection *Heavy Daughter Blues*, these oppressive inscriptions are resultant from State-affiliated hegemons, a national culture of anti-Blackness, and a national culture of misogyny.[45] Coleman's collection signals that these urban tribal scars have an especially insidious way of burrowing beneath gendered Black skin. The poem "Identifying Marks" is a self-inventory of Coleman's bodily markings; its subtle but striking power lies in a tone that is reminiscent of coroner intake notes. Coleman begins her hieroglyphic inventory with:

> raised/black mole 1/4 inch in diameter on nape of left cocoa breast/birthmark/callus on first joint of second finger, right hand/continual rubbings of pencils & pens held too firmly/assorted dark splotches/and patches on hands, neck, arms and backs of legs/stasis dermatitis since birth erupting under acute and chronic stress."[46]

Coleman opens the poem by identifying a raised mole marking her body. Moles are created by skin cells growing in clusters. These melanocyte cells produce melanin, the substance that gives skin its pigmentation.[47] Coleman starts this "identity poem" with a melanin-rich mole, because skin has profoundly marked her life course. Like melanocyte cells, Coleman suggests that many significant experiences have clustered around her racialized body.

The nature of Coleman's signifying mole is seen in its "raised" quality. When a skin lesion (skin that is unlike the skin around it) is raised, it is often accompanied by irritation (i.e., an itchy rash) and extreme discomfort.[48] It is noteworthy that Coleman uses "raised" as a one-word, stand-alone, opening line. The word functions as an introductory adjective to describe the irritation and discomfort Coleman experiences resultant from having gendered Black skin in an anti-Blackness American context. Throughout *Heavy Daughter Blues*, many of Coleman's putatively autobiographical poems explore the discomfiting impact of racism and misogyny on her gendered and racialized body, and on the gendered and racialized bodies of other Black folk. Also, "raise" is a homonym for "raze." The *Oxford English Dictionary* defines "raze": "To scrape (a writing) so as to erase something; to alter by erasure."[49] As a one-word, stand-alone, opening line homonym, Coleman employs "raise" to identify the ways in which virulent anti-Blackness seeks to make Black bodies illegible—and illegitimate. Anti-Blackness *inscribes* hieroglyphics of the flesh to erase Black subjectivity. Anti-Blackness alters racialized subjects so that the remaining traces of Black subjectivity cluster (like raised melanocyte cells) into barely recognizable Black bare life.

Coleman's mole description and its position are noteworthy. Using language reminiscent of a forensic pathologist, the poet describes the black mole as "1/4 inch in diameter on nape of left cocoa breast." Coleman's nomenclature makes the mole sound like a bullet entry wound. The would-be wound is hidden on the nape, the underside of "left cocoa breast." This positioning aligns with the human heart's bodily position. Coleman connects the external, marked mammary gland and the internal, marked endocrine gland. Both glands are capable of sustaining life even when inscribed with hieroglyphics of the flesh. These glands are blues glands. In Coleman's work, the heavy heart and the heavy breast continue to function in the face of adversity. The racialized Black body continues to make a way out of no way. Making a way out of no way is the "birthmark" of the blues.

In response to anti-Blackness's attempt to raze her subjectivity, Coleman raises writing instruments in an attempt to reinscribe that which is in continuous danger of erasure. The poet identifies a specific callus on her writing hand as a resistance marking. It is a resistance marking caused by the "continual rubbings of pencils & pens held too firmly." Coleman meets the continuous danger of erasure with continuous writing. The callus created by this literary response to oppression signifies the labor required to survive. Survival work, liberatory labor, is the kind of work that will make one hold pencils and pens too firmly. Coleman's callus suggests that writing is the type of work that will make one firmly hold on for dear life—especially when one is being pushed toward bare life.

Reading the Body Under Stress

Survival work is stressful work. Along with internal manifestations in the form of high blood pressure rates and heavy heart attack rates, survival stress can manifest externally as skin conditions. Stress is a killer that forewarns its intentions by marking the body. The speaker in Coleman's putatively autobiographical poem "Identifying Marks" has had "stasis dermatitis since birth erupting under acute and chronic stress." Stasis dermatitis is an inflammatory skin disease related to venous hypertension that "typically affects middle-aged and elderly patients, rarely occurring before the fifth decade of life."[50] It is striking that the speaker in "Identifying Marks" has suffered "since birth" from a stress-related skin condition that typically marks the elderly. Poetic license may be providing this early stasis dermatitis onset, but the image and implications are startling. The image of a Black infant emerging from the womb, marked by a stress-related skin condition, hints that the condition was passed from mother to child, that oppression-tethered stress is in the blood. Stasis dermatitis at birth hints that hieroglyphics of the flesh are passed down via platelets.

The second half of "Identifying Marks" highlights the impact of intimate violence on gendered Black bodies. Coleman employs the same forensic pathologist approach as the poem's first half, which gives the poem's second half an even more disturbing tone, because the adversary in question is not only within the speaker's community, but also in her bed. Coleman writes:

> oval indention two cm in diameter on right eye residual from black eye received in fight with first husband over which late night television program to watch slightly puffy right lip with scar on inner tissue busted following duke-out with drunk Louisianan boyfriend who stole ten dollars from purse triangular indention on right pinky, healed scars from cuts received when jumping thru a plate glass window following lover's quarrel beige scar where skin was torn off dorsum of left foot remainder of fist fight which ensued after discovering lover in bed with best friend girl.[51]

The compendium of scars listed above are in the context of intimate relationships. The poem's original page layout includes a space between each "violent episode" described. However, removing the spaces, here, allows the episodes to bleed into each other, echoing bloodletting that the speaker has experienced. Building on Coleman's forensic tone, enumerating individual violence-tethered words in the above excerpt will further elucidate the impact on the marked Black body. In this brief 12-line passage, there are: three scars, two bodily indentions, one busted lip, one cut hand, one skin tear on a foot, and one black eye. Coupling the above violent hieroglyphics with the aforementioned State-sponsored hieroglyphics of the flesh signals that the push toward bare life for Black women is aggressive, comprehensive, and intersectional.

The Intersection of Blues and Abstraction

Legal scholar and Black feminist theorist Kimberlé Crenshaw notes that American courts often refuse to acknowledge the overlapping racial and gender-based claims that Black female plaintiffs raise during discrimination cases.[52] In *DeGraffenreid v. General Motors* (where five Black women claimed the car company discriminated against Black women in hiring, promotion, and retention), Crenshaw writes:

> The court's refusal in *DeGraffenreid* to acknowledge that Black women encounter combined race and sex discrimination implies that the boundaries of sex and race discrimination doctrine are defined respectively by White women's and Black men's experiences . . . Where their experiences are distinct Black women can expect little protection as long as approaches such as that in *DeGraffenreid*, which completely obscure problems of intersectionality, prevail.[53]

Above, Crenshaw writes about the "double-oppression" that Black women often experience. This is a double-oppression that courts implicitly and, at times, explicitly refuse to redress. The juridical message to Black women: choose your gendered self or your racialized self, because we will not adequately address the complex, intersecting, discriminatory sociopolitical forces that impinge upon your life course.

However, this "choose-gender-or-race" message is not confined to the sovereign-sanctioned spatial realm. At times, Black communities and feminists promote a similar message, especially (and ironically) in the liberatory labor context. Crenshaw argues:

> Unable to grasp the importance of Black women's intersectional experiences, not only courts, but, feminists and civil rights thinkers as well have treated Black women in ways that deny both the unique compoundedness of their situation and the centrality of their experiences to the larger classes of women and Blacks . . . Black women's Blackness or femaleness sometimes has placed their needs and perspectives at the margin of the feminist and Black liberationist agendas.[54]

Existing at the margins of a marginalized community, Black women are asked to subvert their own immediate concerns and needs to privilege the concerns and needs of "the community"—which, in practical terms, often manifests as the concerns and needs of Black men. Specifically, Black women writers have, at times, been encouraged not to address intra-community domestic and sexual violence in their creative work, because this creative representation might undermine the "image" of Black men.

In post-Black Power Movement America, a well-known example (and one that moved beyond the academic/activist realm into African-American hush harbors) of Black women being asked to subvert their concerns and needs in favor of the concerns and needs of Black men centered around the publication of Alice Walker's *The Color Purple*. Walker's Pulitzer Prize-winning novel centers around Celie, a domestic and sexual violence survivor (at the hands of Black men, including her father), who goes on a painful, contradiction-filled, but, ultimately emancipatory journey of self-discovery and self-healing.[55] A number of Black male writers and critics took Walker to task for the ways in which the Black male characters were portrayed in the novel. Cultural critic Earl Ofari Huchinson wrote, "Alice Walker's *The Color Purple* finally drove some black men to revolt. Alice named her black man simply 'Mister.' 'Mister' was anyman. He was a misogynist, tyrant, abuser, child beater, and wife beater."[56] Hutchinson lumped Walker (and other African-American female writers including Terry

McMillan and Ntozake Shange who broke silences about intra-Black community domestic and sexual abuse) with European-American men who seemed to have an interest in disparaging Black men and the Black male image. Hutchinson continues, "From slavery to the present, black men listened to White men savage, twist, malign, libel, batter, and mug them in conversation, books and the press . . . But now black women were bad-mouthing them too . . . The things they said about them sounded suspiciously like the same things many White men said about them."[57] For Hutchinson, when Black women writers named intra-community oppression suffered by Black women, the Black women took the form of oppressors. Following Hutchinsonian logic, when Coleman identifies the marks on the Black woman's body, she is victimizing the marker of the Black woman's body.

However, although the speaker in "Identifying Marks" is a Black woman, there are no definitive racial identifiers of the men who marked her body. In the putatively autobiographical poem, racial and literary abstraction meet in the form of the "black eye received in fight with first husband." Coleman's first husband Charlie Coleman was a European American, a Southerner, and a civil rights organizer whose "complexion was sallow, and his naturally curly hair was frizzy on top"—and he often passed for Black.[58] In *Abstractionist Aesthetics*, which argues for the efficacy of abstract-informed Black cultural production and criticism, Phillip Brian Harper avers that Hutchinson's literalist take on Walker's depiction of Black male characters (Hutchinson is also critical of Gloria Naylor's depictions of Black men) is the propelling force behind Hutchinson's critique. Harper writes:

> Hutchinson . . . clearly maintains that what he sees as Shange's, Naylor's, and Walker's unitarily "negative" black male depictions imply that the real world itself holds just one, equally unsympathetic type of black man. It is in this sense that, as I have already intimated, he understands these authors' portrayals of black men as not simply mimetic, or convincingly reflective of real-life black men in their varied individuality, but *emblematic*—that is representative of the general collectivity of black men per se.[59]

Although Coleman's work is rooted in the African-American experience, in Coleman's putatively autobiographical poem "Identifying

Marks," the speaker doesn't identify the races of the men who appear in the poem, so the men who appear in the poem are not "representative of the general collectivity of black men per se." Instead, the speaker is identifying the specific men who marked her body: she is self-witnessing the story of a gendered Black body reinscribed by male hands who sought to change her story and diminish her toward erasure. Following Forché, this poem functions as a poem of witness. "Identifying Marks," as a poem of witness, is a "poem that calls us from the other side of a situation of extremity [so it] cannot be judged by simplistic notions of 'accuracy' or 'truth to life.'" Given a "passing" first husband (Was he passing when he blackened the speaker's eye?) and racially unidentified male lovers, race is an unstable construct vis-à-vis the poem's men. However, what the speaker does definitively identify as Black (in the poem's closing line) is the color of battered "shadows circling eyes."[60] Naming and surviving these hieroglyphics of the flesh that haunt and shadow gendered Black life is the process whereby Coleman creates the poetic sublime. Coleman transforms blues scars into blues poetry. Like Daáood's epigraph that begins this chapter, Wanda Coleman and Kamau Daáood are "uniting the scars to make something beautiful."

Coda

The World Stage Performance Gallery Moves

On Saturday, February 27, 2016, The World Stage Performance Gallery relocated. The announcement of Los Angeles's incoming Crenshaw Rail Line and Leimert Park Station had engendered a buying frenzy in the Crenshaw District's Leimert Park, the Black culture-themed, Degnan Boulevard-centered area. The buying frenzy forced out many long-time merchants. The iconic literary and jazz performance and arts educational center was not offered a lease by the new property owners, so after 27 years at 4344 Degnan Boulevard, The World Stage decided to move—across the street. As opposed to hiring a moving company, Executive Director Dwight Trible decided to organize a moving party in the primarily Latinx and African-American area.[1] Over 50 people showed up. Dozens of primarily Brown and Black people carried congas, computers, microphones, desks, chairs, speakers, paintings, amplifiers, snares, basses, kick drums, and a safe across Degnan Boulevard. The moving sight caused curious motorists to slow and stare.[2]

 The World Stage moving party turnout bespeaks to its status as a grassroots artistic counterpublic in the African-American and Latinx neighborhood. In the context of diminished civic and school arts funding, the non-profit organization's high-quality, low-priced music and literature training brings the community together seven-days-a-week. Offerings include a youth jazz orchestra, all-woman's African drumming workshop and ensemble, a rigorous writing workshop, a jazz vocal workshop, jazz jam sessions, World Stage Press, live jazz concerts, and a children's drumming workshop.³ The multi-ethnic participants are primarily African American and Latinx.

The World Stage is a gathering space to address the sociopolitical and economic challenges facing Black and Brown communities. Although the organization has hosted formal community discussions around police brutality and gentrification, usually, the frequent intra-community discussions occur informally during the literary and music workshops.⁴ These affect-filled discussions are most frequent at the venue's weekly Anansi Writer's Workshop. Participants bring works-in-progress to the poetry-centric workshop, which often addresses issues confronting the Black and Brown communities, including racism, the prison industrial complex, mental health, and violence. The issues embedded in the poetry often arise during the intense feedback process, leading to moving community discussions.

The structure of the workshop contributes to the frequency and intensity of these art-initiated, broad-ranging discussions. Participants who want to workshop a new poem distribute copies to the 30 or 40 people present, then approach the stage to read their poem aloud at the stage's microphone. Following the reading, audience members engage in a lively discussion about the poem's merits and—with very tough love as the guiding principle—its demerits. Audience members are encouraged to publicly disagree with feedback coming from other audience members with whom they have a difference of opinion (giving the poem's author more options to choose from, in terms of making her poem stronger).⁵ This privileging of frank, assertive, democratic discussion, leads to intra-group interrogation, where new ideas and perspectives are welcomed—and challenged. Since the workshop's poetic subject matter is often related to the aforementioned issues confronting Black and Brown communities, The World Stage Anansi Writer's Workshop members engage in an ankhing-tethered process as they collectively think through the most effective means to resist hegemonic forces—and through this idea-exchange, inspire, motivate and move each other toward best practices to resist the circumscription of their subjectivity.

As a writing workshop frequented by labor organizers, published authors, community activists, educators, and neighbors, it is important to note the role literatures play in The World Stage's emancipatory labor. Activists and organizers who attend the workshop are writing and presenting poems about their lives as activists and organizers.

These liberatory laborers' participation in the workshop signals their understanding of the emancipatory possibilities inherent in literatures. Through a democratic and passionate workshop process, they hope to strengthen their cultural labor that it may possibly inspire community members to engage in more emancipatory labor. By writing their own alternative literatures and expanding subjectivity possibilities in the face of hegemonic forces, these labor organizers, published authors, community activists, educators, and neighbors cohere with Edwards assertion that literatures are repositories for "counter stories and alternative visions . . . narrative is a dialogic site for reimagining possibilities."

Notes

Introduction

1. Gloria Anzaldúa, *Borderlands/La Frontera: The New Mestiza* (San Francisco: Aunt Lute Books, 2007), 60.

2. Cedric J. Robinson, *Black Marxisim: The Making of the Black Radical Tradition* (Chapel Hill: University of North Carolina Press, 2000), 310.

3. Ernesto "Che" Guevara, *Socialism and Man in Cuba* (Atlanta, GA: Pathfinder Press, 2009), 24.

4. This study's author was in attendance. There was a multi-racial audience of approximately 75 people, including married owners Oshea and Melanie Luja.

5. "School-to-prison" pipeline is a phrase used to describe the phenomena whereby poorly resourced schools in urban communities increasingly rely on criminalizing methods, such as locker checks, body frisking, handcuffing, and other disciplining actions at the hands of on-campus law enforcement officials. Students at these educational institutions often have negative interactions with the State security apparatus at ages that are extremely problematic. These types of interactions can have the impact of normalizing the criminalization of children.

6. To view video of the rally and McSpadden's response see http://gawker.com/mike-browns-moms-painful-address-to-rally-they-still-1663101735. Accessed Nov. 28, 2014.

7. For a complete list see the report by thinkprogress.org: http://thinkprogress.org/justice/2014/12/12/3601771/people-police-killed-in-2014/. Accessed Jan. 3, 2015.

8. Breanna Edwards, "At Least 5 Black Women Have Died in Police Custody in July." *The Root*, July 30, 2015. *TheRoot.com*. Web. Accessed May 25, 2017.

9. On July 10, 2015, Sandra Bland, 28, was pulled over for a routine traffic stop by Trooper Brian Encina in Waller County, Texas. Video footage

documented the traffic stop escalating after Bland refuses to put out a cigarette in her car. The video shows Encina dragging Bland from her car as she screams in pain. On July 13, 2017, Bland was found hanging in a jail cell in what Waller Country officials defined as a suicide. Bland's family and legal representatives firmly rejected this finding. For more information, see Hayeoun Park's "The Disputed Accounts of the Arrest and Death of Sandra Bland." *New York Times*, July 20, 2015.

10. This study examines sovereign power through a classical lens (the governing body and its representatives right to take life), while incorporating Foucault's biopower concept. Foucault describes biopower as "this technology of the power over 'the' population as such, over men insofar as they are living beings. It is continuous, scientific, and is the power to make live. And now we have the emergence of a power I would call the power of regularization, and it, in contrast, consists of making live and letting die." Michel Foucault, "Society Must Be Defended": *Lectures at the College de France, 1975–76*. Eds. Mauro Bertani and Alessandro Fontana (New York: Picador, 2003), 247.

11. For a survey of Trump's demonizing rhetoric toward women and marginalized groups see Lydia O'Connor and Daniel Marans, "Here are 13 Examples of Donald Trump Being Racist." *The Huffington Post*, Oct. 10, 2016.

12. Giorgio Agamben, *Homo Sacer: Sovereign Power and Bare Life*. Trans. Daniel Heller-Roazen (Palo Alto, CA: Stanford University Press, 1998), 8.

13. Ewa Plonowska Ziarek, *Impasses of the Post-Global: Theory in the Era of Climate Change, Vol. 2*. Ed. Henry Sussman (London: Open Humanities Press, 2012), 195.

14. Alexander G. Weheliye, *Habeous Viscous: Racializing Assemblages, Biopolitics and Black Feminist Theories of the Human* (Durham, NC: Duke University Press, 2014), 4.

15. Weheliye, 4.
16. Ziarek,194–45.
17. Agamben, 8.
18. Agamben, 73.
19. Anzaldúa, 69.

20. Katherine McKittrick, *Demonic Grounds: Black Women and the Cartographies of Struggle* (Minneapolis: University of Minnesota, 2006), 3.

21. According to the *Washington Post* and the *New York Times*, Philando Castile, a 32-year-old nutrition supervisor in Minnesota's St. Paul Public School District was pulled over on a traffic stop in St. Paul suburb Falcon Heights by St. Anthony police officer, 28-year-old, Jeronimo Yanez, on July 6, 2016. Yanez asked for Castile's license and registration. Castile informed Yanez that he had a permit to carry a weapon, which was on his person at the time (Minnesota is a permit-to-carry-firearm state). As Castile

was reaching for his license, Yanez pulled out his service revolver and shot Castile multiple times, killing him. Immediately following the shooting, Diamond Reynolds, passenger and Castile's girlfriend, began live streaming the aftermath on Facebook, showing a slumped and bleeding Castile, and Yanez still pointing his service revolver at Castile. Yanez was charged with 2nd-degree manslaughter and two counts of dangerous discharge of a firearm. On June 16, 2017, Yanez was acquitted of all charges. For more information see Michael Miller, Wesley Lowery, and Lindsay Bever, "Minn. Cop Fatally Shoots Black Man, During Traffic Stop, Aftermath Broadcast on Facebook." *Washington Post*, July 7, 2016, and Mitch Smith, "Minnesota Officer Acquitted in Killing of Philando Castile." *New York Times*, July 6, 2017.

22. According to *The Sacramento Bee* and *The Washington Post* on Sunday night, March 18, 2018, unarmed 22-year-old Stephon Clark was shot at 20 times and killed by two members of the Sacramento Police Department in the backyard of his South Sacramento home that he shared with his grandparents. According to an independent autopsy by famed forensic pathologist Dr. Bennet Omalu, eight of the bullets struck Clark—mostly in the back. Police were in the area responding to a report of an individual breaking car windows near Clark's home. The body camera footage released by the police department does not show police officers identifying themselves as law enforcement officials when they encountered Clark near his home. Clark ran inside his backyard, pursued by the two officers. An officer yelled, "Show me your hands, gun." Within seconds both officers opened fire, killing Clark. There was no gun recovered at the scene. Stephon Clark had been holding a cellphone when he was shot. The phone was found next to his dead body. Anita Chabria, Benjy Egel, and Nashelley Chavez, "Updated: 'Show me your hands.' Police videos show death of Stephon Clark in hail of gunfire." *The Sacramento Bee*, March 22, 2018. Sacbee.com. Web. Accessed March 28, 2018 and Mark Berman, "Stephon Clark was shot eight times, mostly in his back, according to autopsy requested by his family." *The Washington Post*, March 30, 2018. Thewashingtonpost.com. Web. Accessed March 30, 2018.

23. Agamben, 83.

24. Ziarek, 194.

25. This study posits that there are multiple American literatures. However, when referring to highly specific kinds of literature or literature that purports to represent a hegemonic understanding of American literature (i.e., Dead White Men literature), this study will refer to it as American literature or simply literature.

26. See Gordon K. Mantler, *Power to the Poor: Black-Brown Coalition & the Fight for Economic Justice, 1960–1974* (Chapel Hill: University of North Carolina Press, 2013).

27. Toni Cade Bambara, *The Salt Eaters* (New York: Vintage, 2011), 3.

28. See Mel Y. Chen, *Animacies: Biopolitics, Racial Mattering and Queer Affect* (Durham, NC: Duke University Press, 2012); and Jane Bennett, *Vibrant Matter: A Political Ecology of Things* (Durham, NC: Duke University Press, 2010).

29. Chen, 3.

30. Katherine McKittrick, "Mathematics Black Life," *The Black Scholar: Journal of Black Studies and Research* 44 no. 2 (2014): 25.

31. Chen, 2.

32. Chen, 5.

33. Bennett, 20.

34. Sylvia Wynter, "Towards the Sociogenic Principle: Fanon, The Puzzle of Conscious Experience, of 'Identity' and What it's Like to be 'Black,'" 12. Accessed March, 6, 2018. http://coribe.org/PDF/wynter_socio.pdf

35. Wynter, 11.

36. Sylvia Wynter, "Human Being as Noun? Being Human as Praxis? Towards the Autopoetic Turn/Overturn: A Manifesto." Accessed March 4, 2018. https://www.scribd.com/document/329082323/Human-Being-as-Noun-Or-Being-Human-as-Praxis-Towards-the-Autopoetic-Turn-Overturn-A-Manifesto#from_embed

37. Chen, 55.

38. Chen, 47.

39. Bennett, vii.

40. Bennett, 3.

41. Chen, 24.

42. Anzaldúa, 92.

43. This assertion is predicated upon the historical and contemporaneous overrepresentation of White males in American seats of power, including the United States' government's city, county, state, and federal executive, legislative and judicial branches, and leadership positions in the corporate arena.

44. For an engaging discussion of these impacts, tethered to creative narrative, see Sharon Patricia Holland, *Raising the Dead: Readings of Death and (Black) Subjectivity* (Durham, NC: Duke University Press, 2000).

45. Robinson, *Black Marxism*, 121–171, and *Black Movements in America* (New York: Routledge, 1997), 105–111. For further reading see Angela Y. Davis, *Women, Race and Class* (New York: Vintage, 2011) and *Freedom is Constant Struggle: Ferguson, Palestine and the Foundations of a Movement* (Chicago: Haymarket Books, 2016); Robin D. G. Kelley, *Race Rebels: Culture, Politics and the Black Working Class* (New York: The Free Press, 1996) and *Freedom Dreams: The Black Radical Imagination* (Boston: Beacon Press, 2002).

46. Jane Bennett, *The Enchantment of Modern Life: Attachments, Crossings, and Ethics* (Princeton, NJ: Princeton University Press, 2001), 148.

47. In defining the Black spatial imaginary, Lipsitz first juxtaposes it with the White spatial imaginary, which he unpacks in the following way:

"*How Racism Takes Place* argues for the importance of acknowledging the degree to which our society is structured by a White spatial imaginary and for confronting the serious moral, political, and social challenges mounted against it by a [B]lack spatial imaginary. The White spatial imaginary portrays the properly gendered prosperous suburban home as the privileged moral geography of the nation. Widespread, costly, and often counterproductive practices of surveillance, regulation, and incarceration become justified as forms of frontier defense against demonized people of color. Works of popular film and fiction often revolve around phobic representations of Black people unfit for freedom. These cultural commitments have political consequences. They emerge from public policies that place the acquisitive consumer at the center of the social world, that promote hostile privatism and defensive localism as suburban structures of feeling. They encourage homeowners to band together to capture amenities and advantages for themselves while outsourcing responsibilities and burdens to less powerful communities." George Lipsitz, *How Racism Takes Place* (Philadelphia: Temple University Press, 2011), 11. In juxtaposition, the aforementioned White spatial imaginary, Lipsitz defines Black spatial imaginary in the following manner: "The Black spatial imaginary that emerges from complex couplings of race and space promotes solidarities within between and across spaces. . . . The Black spatial imaginary views place as valuable and finite as a public responsibility for which all must take stewardship. Privileging the public good over private interests, this spatial imaginary understands the cost of environmental protection, efficient transportation, affordable housing, public education and universal medical care as common responsibilities to be shared rather than onerous burdens to be palmed off onto the least able and most vulnerable among us." Lipsitz, 69.

48. Lipsitz, 19.

49. *Enchantment*, 136.

50. The author acknowledges the very subjective nature of "good" as concept and telos. For this study, "to do good" can be understood as engaging in behavior that helps historically dispossessed people access heightened agency, more expansive subjectivity, and an improvement in their material conditions, whereby they can more effectively engage in liberatory action.

51. Erica R. Edwards, *Charisma and the Fictions of Black Leadership* (Minneapolis: University of Minnesota Press, 2012), 136.

52. Aihwa Ong, *Neoliberalism as Exception: Mutations in Citizenship and Sovereignty* (Durham, NC: Duke University Press, 2006), 3.

53. Ong, 9.

54. Timothy Brennan,"From development to globalization: postcolonial studies and globalization." *Postcolonial Literary Studies*. Neil Lazarus (Cambridge: Cambridge University Press, 2004), 131.

55. David Harvey, *A Brief History of Neoliberalism* (Oxford: Oxford University Press, 2005), 2.

56. Ankhing is the author's coinage.

57. Nur Ankh Amen, *The Ankh: African Origin of Electromagnetism* (New York: Lushena Books, 1993), 2.

58. Molefi Kete Asante, *The Egyptian Philosophers: Ancient African Voices from Imhotep to Akhenaten* (Chicago: African American Images, 2000), 113. Asante asserts, "[T]o live in Maat is to live in the living Word, the *ankh mdw*. It becomes the only path to *ankh nehen*, that is life eternal."

59. Asante, *The Afrocentric Idea: Revised Edition* (Philadelphia: Temple University Press, 1998), 17. Similarly, Janheinz Jahn argues that "Nommo, the life force, is . . . a unity of spiritual-physical fluidity, giving life to everything, penetrating everything, causing everything. . . . And since man has power over the word, it is he who directs the life force. Through the word he receives it, shares it with other beings, and so fulfills the meaning of life." Janheinz Jahn, *Muntu: African Culture and the Western World* (New York: Grove Press, 1990), 124.

60. "spirit." *Oxforddictionaries.com*. Oxford Dictionaries, 2013. Web. October 28, 2013.

61. Frantz Fanon, *Black Skin, White Masks: Revised Edition* (Grove Press, 2008), 191–92.

62. James H. Cone, *The Spirituals & the Blues* (New York: The Seabury Press, 1972).

63. Cone, 5.

64. Ankhing processes in African-American and Latinx communities often take place in Black and Brown emancipatory sites that, in many cases, would fall within rhetorician Vorris L. Nunley's definition of hush harbors: "Black publics [and this study argues, Brown publics] where Black [and Brown] common sense, 'ideology lived and articulated in everyday understanding of the world and one's place in it,' is assumed to be hegemonic and normative." See Vorris L. Nunley, *Keepin' It Hushed: The Barbershop and African American Hush Harbor Rhetoric* (Detroit, MI: Wayne State University Press, 2011), 36.

65. Cone, 2.

66. Clyde Woods, *Development Arrested: The Blues and Plantation Power in the Mississippi Delta* (Brooklyn: Verso Books, 2017), 30.

67. Michel Foucault, "Society Must Be Defended," *Lectures at the College de France, 1975–76*. Eds. Mauro Bertani and Alessandro Fontana (New York: Picador, 2003), 247. Michel Foucault defines biopower in opposition to sovereign power, the power to "take life." Foucault describes biopower as "this technology of the power over 'the' population as such, over men insofar as they are living beings. It is continuous, scientific, and is the power to make

live. And now we have the emergence of a power I would call the power of regularization, and it, in contrast, consists of making live and letting die."

68. Orlando Patterson, *Slavery and Social Death: A Comparative Study* (Cambridge, MA: Harvard University Press, 1982), 5. In writing about slaves' material and, concomitant, social condition, Patterson asserts, "He was truly a genealogical isolate. Formally isolated in his social relations with those who lived, he also was culturally isolated from the social heritage of his ancestors." Cone suggests that the Spirit has the power to reject this social death, and use this rejection to create a more vibrant mode of living.

69. Cone, 5.

70. Woods presents blues epistemology in the following manner, "[W]orking-class African Americans in the Delta and the Black Belt South have constructed a system of explanation that informs their daily life, organizational activity, culture, religion and social movements. They have created their own ethno-regional epistemology. Like other traditions of interpretation, it is not a monolith; there are branches, roots, and a trunk. This central tradition is referred to in this work as the blues epistemology." Woods, 16.

71. Woods, 17.

72. Fred Moten, *In the Break: The Aesthetics of the Black Radical Tradition* (Minneapolis: The University of Minnesota Press, 2003), 22.

73. Cone, 5.

74. For a thorough examination of Hegel's impact on racism's development see Teshale Tibebu, *Hegel and the Third World: The Making of Eurocentrism in World History* (Syracuse, NY: Syracuse University Press, 2011).

75. G. W. F. Hegel, *The Philosophy of Art*. Trans. William Hastie (New York: Barnes & Noble, 2006), 4.

76. Audre Lorde, *Sister Outsider: Essays and Speeches* (New York: Ten Speed Press, 2007), 53–56.

77. Lorde, 56.

78. Hans Christian Von Baeyer, *Warmth Disperses and Time Passes: The History of Heat* (New York: The Modern Library, 1999), 14–18.

79. In *Charisma*, Edwards's devastating critique of African-American historic and contemporary deification of the charismatic male leader as a salvific instrument of Black communities, she theorizes that "as a structuring fiction for liberatory politics, charisma is founded in three forms of violence: the historical or historiographical violence of reducing a heterogeneous black freedom struggle to a top-down narrative of Great Man leadership; the social violence of performing social change in the form of a fundamentally anti-democratic form of authority; and the epistemological violence of structuring knowledge of black political subjectivity and movement within a gendered hierarchy of political value that grants uninterrogated power to normative masculinity" (xv).

80. Edwards, xv.

81. See Barbara Smith's "Where's the Revolution" in *The Truth That Never Hurts: writings on race, gender and freedom* (New Brunswick, NJ: Rutgers University Press, 1998).

82. Frances Beale, "Double Jeopardy: To Be Black and Female," *The Black Woman* (New York: New American Library, 1970), 93.

83. Toni Cade (Bambara), ed. *The Black Woman* (New York: New American Library, 1970), 102–03.

84. Smith, 179–80.

85. Jean Bond and Patricía Peery, *The Black Woman*, 114.

86. Sharon Patricia Holland, *Raising the Dead: Readings of Death and (Black) Subjectivity* (Durham, NC: Duke University Press, 2000), 108.

87. For more reading on the topic see Gloria T. Hull, Patricia Bell Scott, and Barbara Smith, eds. *All the Women Are White, All the Blacks Are Men, But Some of Us Are Brave: Black Women's Studies* (New York: The Feminist Press at City University of New York, 1982); Kevin J. Mumford, "Homo Sex Changes: Race, Cultural Geography, and the Emergence of the Gay," *American Quarterly* 48, no. 3 (1996): 395–414; Suzanne Pharr, *Homophobia: A Weapon of Sexism* (Berkeley, CA: Chardon Press, 1997); Diana Fuss, *Essentially Speaking: Feminism, Nature, and Difference* (New York: Routledge, 1989); Alice Echols, *Daring to Be Bad: Radical Feminism in America 1967–1975* (Minneapolis: University of Minnesota Press, 1989; Mab Segrest, *Memoir of a Race Traitor* (Boston: South End Press, 1993); Michael Awkward, *Negotiating Difference: Race, Gender and the Politics of Positionality* (Chicago: University of Chicago Press, 1995); Audre Lorde, *Sister Outsider: Essays and Speeches* (Berkeley: Crossings Press, 1984); Robert McRuer, "A Visitation of Difference: Randall Kenan and Black Queer Theory," *Journal of Homosexuality* 26, nos. 2 and 3 (1993): 221–32.

88. For further reading on the ancient Egyptian spiritual system see Ra Un Nefer Amen I, *Metu Neter Vol. 1: The Great Oracle of Tehuti and the Egyptian System of Spiritual Cultivation* (Brooklyn: Kamit Publications, 1990); Fracois R. Herbin, *Books of Breathing and Related Texts, Vol. 4* (London: British Museum Press, 2008); E. A. Wallis Budge, *The Egyptian Book of the Dead* (Mineola, NY: Dover Publications, 1967); Adolph Erman, *Life in Ancient Egypt* (Mineloa, NY: Dover Publications, 1971).

89. Moraga, 100.

90. For an exploration of this patriarchal, Great Man, top-down leadership-style in emancipatory labor see Edwards, 3–33.

91. Jürgen Habermas, *The Structural Transformation of the Public Sphere: An Inquiry into a Category of Bourgeois Society*. Trans. Thomas Burger (Cambridge: MIT Press, 1991).

92. Habermas, 2.

93. Habermas, 30–32.

94. Nancy Fraser, "Rethinking the Public Sphere: A Contribution of the Critique of Actually Existing Democracy," *Social Text* 25/26 (1990): 67.

95. Laura Pulido, *Black, Brown, Yellow and Left: Radical Activism in Los Angeles* (Berkeley: University of California Press, 2016), 117.

96. Pulido, 121.

97. Pulido, 117–46.

98. Maylei Blackwell, *Chicana Power!: Contested Histories of Feminism in the Chicano Movement* (Austin: University of Texas Press, 2011), 11.

99. Catherine R. Squires, "Rethinking the Black Public Sphere: An Alternative Vocabulary for Multiple Public Spheres," *Communication Theory* 12:4 (2002): 458.

100. Squires, 460.

101. Margaret Kohn, *Radical Space: Building the House of the People* (Ithaca, NY: Cornell University Press, 2003), 91.

102. Michel Foucault, "Of Other Spaces," *Rethinking Architecture: A Reader in Cultural Theory*. Ed. Neal Leach (New York: Routledge, 1997), 352.

103. See Michel Foucault, "Different Spaces" *Michel Foucault: Aesthetics, Method and Epistemology*. Ed. James Faubion (New York: The New Press, 1998), 175–85.

104. Kohn, 129.

105. Kohn, 129.

106. According to Kohn, in her research investigating European heterotopias of resistance dedicated to supporting workers, socialists and communists in the 18th and early 19th centuries, houses of the people were "simultaneously pragmatic solutions to police harassment and surveillance, attempts to embody solidarity, and intervention in the symbolic space of the city. They challenged political and economic structures because they functioned as material and symbolic nodal points for aggregating dispersed people and ideas," (88).

107. Kohn, 151.

108. Kohn, 152.

109. Kohn, 152.

110. Kohn, 152.

111. Cone, 5.

112. Lorde, 53.

113. Kohn, 129.

114. Toni Cade Bambara, *The Salt Eaters* (New York: Vintage Books, 1980).

115. Lawrence P. Jackson, *The Indignant Generation: A Narrative History of African American Writers and Critics, 1934–1960* (Princeton, NJ: Princeton University Press, 2011), 29–30.

116. Duchess Harris, "From the Kennedy Commission to the Combahee Collective: Black Feminist Organizing, 1960–1980," *Sisters in the Struggle: African American Women in the Civil Rights-Black Power Movement.* Eds. Bettye Collier-Thomas and V. P. Franklin (New York: NYU Press, 2001), 282–305. Harris argues that there is a through-line from the Fourth Consultation of President John F. Kennedy's Commission on the Status of Women (PCSW) to those of the women in the National Black Feminist Organization (NBFO) and the Combahee River Collective (CRC). Harris theorizes that "The first group was composed of financially and educationally privileged black women chosen by officials of the federal government to serve on a national commission on women, while the other two included middle- and working-class black women who had been active in civil rights and grassroots black organizations.

This study examines the political activities of these Black women and their organizations, and reveals that despite differences in education and social class background, they were aware of three overlapping realities: (1) there were inextricable links between gender and racial identify; (2) their socioeconomic status was overdetermined by gender and racial identity; and (3) there was a need to organize collectively on the basis of these realizations.

This research reveals that each group's ideological perspectives were more inclusive than those of their predecessors. The black women on the Kennedy Commission articulated more conservative notions about gender than the women of the National Black Feminist Organization (NBFO) who, in turn, articulated more conservative notions about female sexuality and the disadvantages of the capitalist system than the women of the Combahee River Collective. Unlike the women of the Kennedy Commission and the NBFO, those members of the Combahee River Collective recognized that one's sexual orientation was distinctive and separate from gender and racial identity and they organized around that realization.

The Black Feminist Movement can be seen as moving from relatively liberal and univocal focus on gender of the Presidential Commission to the more radical and polyvocal focus on gender, race, class, and sexual orientation of the Combahee River Collective. This study makes it clear that the later groups existed as a result of the efforts of the earlier ones, and that there was significant overlap in membership. Moreover, the ideological development among Black feminists coincided with the growth of the Civil Rights-Black Power and Women's Liberation Movements, to which they made important contributions" (282).

117. Harris, 288.
118. Harris, 292–93.
119. Harris, 293.
120. Harris, 282–93.
121. Arthur F. Redding, *Haints: American Ghosts, Millennial Passions, and Contemporary Gothic Fictions* (Tuscaloosa: University of Alabama Press), 9.

122. Frederick Douglass, *Narrative of the Life of Frederick Douglass, An American Slave* (Hollywood, FL: Simon and Brown, 2013), 29.

123. Douglass, 29.

124. Vorris L. Nunley, *Keepin' It Hushed: The Barbershop and African American Hush Harbor Rhetoric* (Detroit, MI: Wayne State University Press, 2011), 36. Although the African American Hush Harbor can inform our understanding of hush harbor-like spatial constructions and their associated mores and folkways in Latinx communities, I acknowledge that the imbrication in this relationship creates slippage as I attempt to apply an African-American culturally-centric epistemic tool to Latinx communities.

125. For a comprehensive examination of this relationship see Gordon K. Mantler, *Power to the Poor: Black-Brown Coalition & the Fight for Economic Justice, 1960–1974* (Chapel Hill: University of North Carolina Press, 2013).

126. Lipsitz, 42.

Chapter 1

1. Salvador Plascencia, *The People of Paper* (New York: Harvest Books, 2006), 219.

2. Ishmael Reed, *Mumbo Jumbo* (New York: Scribner, 1972), 183.

3. "Cut." Def. 1. *The Compact Edition of the Oxford English Dictionary*, 1997.

4. "Cut." Def. 1.

5. Fred Moten, *In the Break: The Aesthetics of the Black Radical Tradition* (Minneapolis: University of Minnesota Press, 2003), 70.

6. Plascencia, 84.

7. Plascenica, 34.

8. Plascencia, 34.

9. Plascencia, 53.

10. Plascencia, 53.

11. Moten, 239.

12. Plascencia, 53.

13. Karl Marx, "Estranged Labor," *The Marx-Engels Reader, 2nd Edition*. Ed. Robert C. Tucker (New York: Norton & Company, 1978), 74.

14. Plascencia, 68.

15. Plascencia, 65.

16. Plascencia, 55.

17. Plascencia, 54.

18. Plascencia, 85.

19. Plascencia, 85.

20. Reed, 204.

21. Reed, 204.

22. Moten, 256.

23. Bruno Latour, *Pandora's Hope: Essays on the Reality of Science Studies* (Cambridge, MA: Harvard University Press, 1999), 281.

24. Henry Louis Gates, Jr., *The Signifying Monkey: A Theory of Afro-American Literary Criticism* (New York: Oxford University Press, 1988), 235.

25. Kamau Daáood, *The Language of Saxophones: Selected Poems of Kamau Daáood* (San Francisco: City Lights, 2005), 35.

26. Bennett, 63–65.

27. Bennett, 63.

28. Bennett, 77.

29. Cone, 5.

30. Bennett, 66.

31. Reed, 64.

32. For interesting examinations of socially-engaged artists in social movements see Gay Theresa Johnson, *Spaces of Conflict, Sounds of Solidarity: Music, Race and Spatial Entitlement in Los Angeles* (Berkeley: University of California Press, 2013); Robin D. G. Kelley, *Race Rebels: Culture, Politics and the Black Working Class* (New York: The Free Press, 1994); and, Harry J. Elam, Jr., *Taking It to the Streets: The Social Protest Theater of Luis Valdez and Amiri Baraka*.

33. Cone suggests that in the blues music context, heightened social justice commitment can manifest as a heightened will to survive virulent anti-Blackness, which can be a positive externality of disenfranchised folk communing around the blues, 133–37; Johnson's *Spaces of Conflict, Sounds of Solidarity* is especially insightful about the ways in which music operates as social justice actant, specifically, in the Latinx and African-American context.

34. Reed, 63.

35. Reed, 82.

36. Two representative examples of this phenomena are Ghanaian independence leader Kwame Nkrumah who was educated at the University of Pennsylvania and Lincoln University and Nigerian activist-playwright Wole Soyinka who did graduate study at the University of Leeds in Britain.

37. This study refers to Africa and African, however, it acknowledges the folkways, mores, and specific cultures of individual African countries, tribes and the people therein.

38. For an interesting look at the role of dominoes in Latinx culture see *Franciso Lomelí, ed. Handbook of Hispanic Cultures in the United States: Literature and Art* (Houston: Arte Público Press, 1993), 241–42.

39. Plascencia, 55.

40. Dan Tracy. "Dominoes: A Link to Heritage for Many Hispanics in U.S." *The Orlando Sentinel*, June 28, 2000. SunSentinel Web. May 18, 2015.

41. Tracy "Dominoes."

42. Dominologists are not only skilled in the art of playing the game, they are also skilled in the artful word-play exchanged among players during games. See *Nathan Holsey, The Dominologist: Learn to Become the Best at Dominoes* (Bloomington, IL: iUniverse, 2008).

Chapter 2

1. Hortense J. Spillers, "Mama's Baby, Papa's Maybe: An American Grammar Book." *Diacritics* (Summer, 1987): 67.
2. Spillers, 67.
3. Spillers, 68.
4. Spillers uses this term to describe the ways in which Black flesh is seared, divided, and ripped apart.
5. Spillers 67.
6. Alexander G. Weheliye, *Habeous Viscous: Racializing Assemblages, Biopolitics and Black Feminist Theories of the Human* (Durham: Duke University Press, 2014), 39–40.
7. Fraser 67.
8. Squires 460.
9. Kohn 129.
10. Moraga 89.
11. Moraga 133.
12. Moraga 110.
13. Moraga 129.
14. Weheliye 158.
15. Jacques Derrida, *Rogues: Two Essays on Reason*. Trans. Pascale-Anne Brault and Michael Naas (Palo Alto: Stanford University Press, 2005), 100.
16. Audre Lorde, *Sister Outsider: Essays and Speeches* (New York: Ten Speed Press, 2007), 41.
17. Michel Foucault, *The History of Sexuality, Volume 1: an introduction* (New York: Knopf, 1990), 27.
18. Moraga 111–112.
19. Moraga 96.
20. Moraga 92.
21. Moraga 130.
22. Moraga 130.
23. Foucault, *The History of Sexuality*. 27.
24. Kohn 129.
25. Moraga 92–94.
26. Moraga 148.

27. The especially ardent embrace by Mexican migrants of la Virgen de Guadalupe seems to be tethered to the anxieties inherent in the process of leaving the homeland to pursue economic survival. For an intriguing treatment of how la Virgen de Guadalupe functions as a central religious figure of worship for Mexican migrants, including the intensity of the embrace, see Elaine A. Pena, *Performing Piety: Making Space Sacred with the Virgin of Guadalupe* (University of California, 2011).

28. Moraga 148.

29. Yvonne Yarbo-Bejarano, *The Wounded Heart: Writing on Cherríe Moraga* (Austin: University of Texas Press, 2001), 76.

30. Moraga 149.

31. Moraga 149.

32. Moraga 149.

33. Moraga 149.

34. For an incisive critical history of community organizing, including case studies that illustrate the import of engaging community members as the experts on changing their own communities see David Walls, *Community Organizing* (Cambridge: Polity Press, 2015).

35. Lorde 56.

36. Moraga 102.

37. Moraga 102.

38. Moraga 102–103.

39. Moraga 124.

40. For the foundational text in the study and application of liberation theology see Gustavo Gutiérrez, A *Theology of Liberation: History Politics and Salvation*. Trans. Caridad Inda (Ossining: Orbis Books, 1988).

41. Moraga 115.

42. Moraga 130.

43. For an authoritative critical study of the history and myth-making around the Passion see John Dominic Crossan, *The Cross That Spoke: The Origins of the Passion Narrative* (New York: Harper Collins, 1992).

44. Moraga 135.

45. Moraga 149.

46. Moraga 144.

47. Moraga 149.

Chapter 3

1. Moraga's Barbara Smith-related "we're sisters" quote that starts this chapter is also a revisioning of socioreligious doctrine. *This Bridge Called My Back* and *June Jordan's Poetry for the People* represent new forms of sacred

texts. These are texts calling for a belief in liberatory bridges across race, class, and sexual orientation in the name of justice. These two revolutionary anthologies encourage faith in activists and their salvific sacrificial labor. Moraga ends the aforementioned preface by affirming her faith in sacred activist work: "[Faith] helped me continue the labor of this book. I am not talking about some lazy faith . . . I am talking about believing that we have the power to actually transform our experience, change our lives, save our lives. Otherwise, why this book? It is the faith of activists I am talking about."[53] Toni Cade Bambara, *This Bridge Called My Back: Writings by Radical Women of Color*. Eds. Cherríe L. Moraga and Gloria E. Anzaldua (Berkeley, CA: Third Woman Press, 2002), xlii.

    2. Brent Hayes Edwards, *The Practice of Diaspora: Literature, Translation, and the Rise of Black Internationalism* (Cambridge, MA: Harvard University Press, 2003), 45.

    3. *This Bridge*, xlv.

    4. "shock." Def. 4. *The Compact Edition of the Oxford English Dictionary*. vol. 2. 1971.

    5. See Shelby Steele, *The Content of Our Character: A New Vision of Race in America* (New York: Harper Perennial, 1998). The color-blind discourse ignited by Steele has been effectively nurtured by conservative thinkers like William Kristol and conservative media commentators like Bill O'Reilly.

    6. Margaret Kohn, *Radical Space: Building the House of the People* (Ithaca, NY: Cornell University Press, 2003), 91.

    7. Kohn, 129.

    8. Blackwell, 134.

    9. Along with Moraga and Anzaldúa, contributors include Audre Lorde, Barbara Smith, Merle Woo, Beverly Smith, Cheryl Clarke, Mitsuye Yamada, Naomi Littlebear Morena, Rosario Morales, Chrystos, Norma Alarcón, Nellie Wong, and Jo Carrillo, among others.

    10. Angela Y. Davis, *This Bridge*. Back cover.

    11. Jane Bennett, *Vibrant: A Political Ecology of Things* (Durham, NC: Duke University Press, 2010), vii.

    12. Kohn, 129. Kohn's use of the term is part of a larger class analysis. Kohn argues that workers need safe havens to provide cover from an atomizing, capitalist sovereign's gaze, which seeks to delimit their identity to cogs in profit-maximization machinery. Generally, the imbricated nature of American class and race makes Kohn's safe haven notion productive when discussing Black and Brown folk's need for cover from the atomizing gaze of American neoliberal sovereigns.

    13. *This Bridge*, lii.

    14. *This Bridge*, lii.

    15. *This Bridge*, lii.

16. Nancy Fraser, "Rethinking the Public Sphere: A Contribution of the Critique of Actually Existing Democracy," *Social Text* 25/26 (1990): 67.

17. June Jordan, *June Jordan's Poetry for the People: A Revolutionary Blueprint*. Eds. Lauren Muller and the Blueprint Collective (New York: Routledge, 1995), 4.

18. Lipsitz, 60.

19. Barbara Christian, "Being the Subject and the Object" in *New Black Feminist Criticism, 1985–2000*. Eds. Bowles, Gloria, M. Giulia Fabi, and Arlene R. Keizer. Urbana: University of Illinois Press, 2007), 122.

20. Jordan, 69. Jordan writes about rescuing the canon in terms of reinventing it and making it relevant for the living by honoring the diverse work of the living as well as the dead.

21. Catherine R. Squires, "Rethinking the Black Public Sphere: An Alternative Vocabulary for Multiple Public Spheres," *Communication Theory* 12:4 (2002): 460.

22. Lauren Muller, *June Jordan's Poetry for the People*, 228.

23. Adrienne Rich, "Writing with the Sun," *June Jordan's Poetry for the People*, 80.

24. Marilyn Chin, *June Jordan's Poetry for the People*, 83.

25. Chin's critically-acclaimed poetry and outspoken advocacy for the "survival" of her work has began to make inroads. Chin's poems are now included in the canon-influencing anthologies: *The Norton Anthology of Literature by Women*, *The Norton Introduction to Poetry*, and *The Oxford Anthology of Modern American Poetry*.

26. Chin, *June Jordan's Poetry for the People*, 83.

27. Jordan, *June Jordan's Poetry for the People*, 5.

28. Paulo Freire, *Pedagogy of the Oppressed* (New York: Continuum, 1996), 17. This is Myra Bergman Ramos's translation of the term.

29. *June Jordan's Poetry for the People*, 36. Also, this definition includes: "The achievement of maximum impact with minimal number of words" and "The utmost precision in the use of language, hence, density and intensity of expression."

30. Freire, 68.

31. *June Jordan's Poetry for the People*, 17.

32. Freire, 69.

33. Mel Y. Chen, *Animacies: Biopolitics, Racial Mattering and Queer Affect* (Durham, NC: Duke University Press, 2012), 30.

34. Freire, 69.

35. Freire, 53.

36. This term is the author's coinage. The coinage refers to the process involving the relatively powerful hailing the relatively less powerful with pejoratives meant to denigrate and delimit subjectivity.

37. Chen, 31.

38. Chen, 31. Sidarth's video of Allen's comment was uploaded to You Tube and soon went viral. See https://www.youtube.com/watch?v=r90z0PMnKwI

39. Chen, 32.

40. Chen, 34–35. Chen argues that the media coverage of the Allen/Sidarth encounter doesn't sufficiently challenge the underlying assumptions that there is not a horizontal relationship between humans and simians. The following quote offers a glimpse into Chen's position: [A] simian imputation for a human being readily invokes theories of evolution that place monkeys and apes a earlier, "primitive," stages of evolution or development than the, "higher," humans being compared to them."

41. Lisa Lowe, *Immigrant Acts: On Asian American Cultural Politics* (Durham, NC: Duke University Press, 1996), 14–17.

42. Lowe, 10–14.

43. Lowe, 27. Lowe argues that naturalization involves a false promise of sociopolitical emancipation and equality: "While the nation proposes immigrant 'naturalization' as a narrative of political emancipation that is meant to resolve in American liberal democracy as a terrain to which all citizens have equal access and in which all are equally represented, it is a narrative that denies the establishment of citizenship out of unequal relationships between dominant White citizens and subordinated racialized noncitizens and women."

44. Lowe, 26–27.

45. Chen, 35.

46. *The Washington Post* staff. "Donald Trump Announces a Presidential Bid: Full Text. *The Washington Post*. June 16, 2015. Web. Accessed Feb. 12, 2016.

47. Further entrenching the conflict and document in irony, the Treaty of Guadalupe Hidalgo was officially entitled the "Treaty of Peace, Friendship, Limits and Settlement between the United States of America and the Mexican Republic." Richard Griswold del Castillo argues that as soon as 1849 the ambiguous, interpretative, and fluid nature of race began to play a role in how the treaty was enforced, especially as the framers of California's constitution began to wrestle with the intersection of race, rights of citizenship, and the Treaty of Guadalupe Hidalgo. For more on this discussion see Richard Griswold del Castillo, *The Treaty of Guadalupe Hidalgo* (Norman: University of Oklahoma Press, 1990), 62–86.

48. Griswold del Castillo, 66.

49. Griswold del Castillo, 66.

50. Gwenda Blair, *The Trumps: Three Generations of Builders* (New York: Simon & Schuster, 2001), 94.

51. Moraga, xxiv.

52. Max Wolf Valerio, "It's in My Blood, My Face—My Mother's Voice, the Way I Sweat." *This Bridge*, 41.

Chapter 4

1. Kamau Daáood, "The Lip Drummer." *The Language of Saxophones: Selected Poems of Kamau Daáood* (San Francisco: City Lights Books, 2005), 25.

2. "True word" is commonly heard, vernacular usage in the Black church to reference bible material.

3. *New International Version*, Mark 4:1006–17.

4. This traditional Black benediction is drawn from the biblical narrative that details a truce between Laban and Jacob: "May the Lord keep watch between you and me when we are away from each other." *New International Version*, Genesis 31:49.

5. Elizabeth Chuck. "Charleston Church Shooter Dylan Roof 'Caught Us With Our Eyes Closed'" including interview transcript. *NBCNews.com*. NBC News, September 10, 2015. Web. 2 March 2016.

6. "Charleston Church Shooter."

7. "Charleston Church Shooter."

8. "Charleston Church Shooter."

9. "Charleston Church Shooter." The seven other victims were South Carolina state senator and Emanuel African Methodist Episcopalian Church senior pastor Rev. Clementa Pinckney, Rev. Sharonda Singleton, Rev. Daniel Simmons, Rev. DePayne Middlton-Doctor, Myra Thompson, Ethel Lance, and Cynthia Hurd.

10. Frances Robles. "Dylan Roof Photos and a Manifesto Are Posted on a Website." *Newyorktimes.com. New York Times*. June 20, 2015. Web. March 3, 2016.

11. Jerod Sexton, "Unbearable Blackness." *Cultural Critique* 90 (Spring 2015): 159.

12. CNN Newsroom. "Transcript: Prayer Vigil Planned; Dylann Roof Hearing." *CNN.com*. CNN. June 19, 2015. Web. March 3 2016.

13. James H. Cone, *The Spirituals & the Blues* (New York: The Seabury Press, 1972), 5.

14. As a founding member of the surrealist movement, André Bretons argued that one of the movement's defining ideals was that "two distant realities" can unite to form a new reality. Jesús Benito Sánchez, Ana M. Manzanas, and Begoña Simal aver that this defining element of surrealism echoes the experience of colonized Latinx and African Americans. As a result, the trio suggest that Black and Brown lives, themselves, can be surreal: "André Breton's narrative juxtaposition of 'two more or less distant realities' in the Paris of the 1920s aptly epitomizes the unwanted but inevitable state of mind

of postcolonial communities in Africa and Asia after the demise of colonial empires. The straddling of two remote cultures, with their concomitant cross-pollination, is generally recognized as a distinctive mark of many postcolonial societies. The mestizo nature of most postcolonial cultures results in the frequent presentation of dualities and juxtapositions, the 'double consciousness' that Du Bois explored in the African American experience." See Jesús Benito Sánchez, Ana M. Manzanas, and Begoña Simal. *Uncertain Mirrors: Magical Realisms in US Ethnic Literatures* (Amsterdam: Editions Rodopi, 2009), 110. In this context, Daáood's poetry, which features odd juxtapositions of images and realities, places him squarely in the surrealist tradition.

15. Kamau Daáood, "Army of Healers." *The Language of Saxophones: Selected Poems of Kamau Daáood* (San Francisco: City Lights Books, 2005), 57.

16. James Baldwin, "The Struggle." Buddha Records,1969. Vinyl. The recording is of a 1963 speech Baldwin gave in New York City.

17. Daáood, 57.

18. Matthew Arnold, "The Study of Poetry." *Classic Writings on Poetry*. Ed. William Harmon (New York: Columbia University Press, 2005), 464.

19. Daáood, 57.

20. Daáood, 58.

21. According to business research firm IBISWorld, in 2015 the United States' floral industry created six billion dollars in revenue. There were 35,343 floral businesses, employing 83,208 workers. See "Florists in the US: Market Research Report." *IBISWorld.com*. December 2015. Web. March 9, 2016.

22. Carolyn Forché sees value in considering the spatial and sociopolitical context when adjudicating a poem's significance. Forché argues, "By situating poetry in this social space, we can avoid some of our residual prejudices. A poem that calls us from the other side of a situation of extremity cannot be judged by simplistic notions of 'accuracy' or 'truth to life.' It will have to be judged, as Ludwig Wittgenstein said of confession, by its consequences, not by our ability to verify its truth. In fact, the poem might be our only evidence that an event has occurred: it exists for us as the sole trace of an occurrence. As such, there is nothing for us to base the poem on, no independent account that will tell us whether or not we can see a given text as being 'objectively' true. Poem as trace, poem as evidence." Forché's argument also suggests that not only is the poem evidence, but so is the poet who creates the poem as evidence. Carolyn Forché, "Twentieth Century Poetry of Witness." *American Poetry Review* 22:2 (March–April 1993), 9–16.

23. Daáood, 58.

24. Woods, 25.

25. Daáood, 59.

26. Walter Johnson, *River of Dark Dreams: Slavery and Empire in the Cotton Kingdom* (Cambridge, MA: Harvard University Press, 2013), 244.

27. Johnson, 279.

28. Daáood, 59.

29. See G. M. Wassel and N. M. Ammar, "Isolation of the Alkaloids and Evaluation of the Diuretic Activity of Arundo Donax." *Fitoterapia* 15:6 (1984): 357–58, and Giuseppe Tagarelli, Antonio Tagarelli, and Anna Piro, "Folk Medicine to Heal Malaria in Calabria." *Journal of Ethnobiology and Ethnomedicine* 6 (2010): 27.

30. Robert E. Perdue, "Arundo Donax—Source of Musical Reeds and Industrial Cellulose. *Economic Botany* 12:4 (Oct.–Dec. 1958), 377–79. As Salih Gücel argues, following Perdue, the modern technological advancements have not been able to find a more effective material to use for reeds than these plants that were once used in the religious wrapping of mummies in 4th Century A.D. Egypt. See Salih Gücel, "Arundo Donax L. Giant Reeds Use By Turkish Cypriots." *Ethnobotany* 8 (2010), 245–48.

31. Fred Moten, *In the Break: The Aesthetics of the Black Radical Tradition* (Minneapolis: The University of Minnesota Press, 2003), 22.

32. Daáood, 59.

33. Daáood, 59.

34. Centers for Disease Control and Prevention. "A Closer Look at African American Men and High Blood Pressure Control: A Review of Psychosocial Factors and Systems-Level Interventions." U.S. Department of Health and Human Services (Atlanta, 2010), 7–9.

35. Hortense J. Spillers, "Mama's Baby, Papa's Maybe: An American Grammar Book." *Diacritics* (Summer, 1987): 67.

36. Daáood, 59.

37. Daáood, 59.

38. Daáood, 60.

39. Daáood, 60.

40. Daáood, 60.

41. Daáood, 60.

42. Daáood, 60.

43. Although the interpretation that the 14th Amendment's use of "person" includes corporations (in some regards) is generally accepted within the legal community, there is still resistance to the idea among some legal scholars. For a compelling argument against the "corporations as persons" interpretation see Carl Meyer, "Personalizing the Impersonal: Corporations and the Bill of Rights." *Hastings Law Journal* 41:3 (March 1990).

44. Daáood, 60.

45. Wanda Coleman, *Heavy Daughter Blues: Poems & Stories 1968–1986* (Santa Rosa, CA: Black Sparrow Press, 1987).

46. Coleman, 198.

47. The Mayo Clinic Staff "Diseases-Conditions-Moles-Basics-Causes." Mayoclinic.org. www.mayoclinic.org. December 6, 2014. Web. March 26, 2016.

48. "Diseases-Conditons."

49. "Raze." Entry 4a. *The Compact Edition of the Oxford English Dictionary* (Oxford: Oxford University Press, 1979).

50. Scott Flugman, "Stasis Dermatitis." *Medscape*. Medscape.com. March 7, 2016. Web. March 27, 2016.

51. Coleman, 198.

52. Kimberlé Crenshaw, "Demarginalizing the Intersection of Race and Sex: A Black Feminist Critique of Antidiscrimination Doctrine, Feminist Theory and Ant-Racist Politics." *The University of Chicago Legal Forum* (1989): 139–68.

53. Crenshaw, 143.

54. Crenshaw, 150.

55. Alice Walker, *The Color Purple* (New York: Mariner Books, 2003). The controversy around the novel's publication played out amidst a national discourse in the 1980s around the idea of Black men as an "endangered species," given their incarceration rates and consistently disturbing socioeconomic and health indicator numbers.

56. Earl Ofari Hutchinson, *The Assassination of the Black Male Image* (New York: Simon Schuster, 1996), 104.

57. Hutchinson, 103.

58. Wanda Coleman, *The Riot Inside Me: More Trials & Tremors* (Jaffrey, NH: Black Sparrow Books, 2005), 30–39. A mix of memoir and new journalism, Coleman's nonfiction collection includes a recounting of her life with European-American Southerner Charles Coleman. The relationship offers a glimpse into how difficult it is to place Coleman, her work and her relationships, especially with European Americans, into neat categories defined by race. A complicated man, Coleman self-identified as a "redneck" and "peckerwood" but was a committed civil rights activist who had been jailed and beaten for his activism. They married when Wanda and Charlie Coleman were 18 and 22, respectively. Wanda Coleman writes about her first husband, who passed for Black—and putatively gave her a Black eye in "Identifying Marks: "[Charlie] enjoyed being a black man. What had begun as a simple ploy soon became an elaborate deception. On the Black-hand-side of life, we frequented the paranoiac gatherings of political and cultural activists, and even donned dress clothes to attend the mosques—Orthodox and Black Muslim. Whenever his authenticity was questioned, Charlie reveled in proving he had forgotten more about being Black than his challengers had ever known. During one nasty showdown, he mollified the majority of the skeptics, but the atmosphere remained threatening. Someone put James Brown on the stereo as the ultimate test. Charlie could bop, camel walk and Madison, he could do the dog, the funky butt, and the alligator crawl. His dance performance dispelled all remaining doubts. Whenever challenged to

unzip his fly, he did so with pride. Once three hardcore bruthas escorted him to the john. They returned in consternation, embarrassed. Quick to drop his drawers, Charlie would never remove his shirt, mindful to keep cuffed sleeves just about the elbow, hiding that Johnny Reb tattoo. I never betrayed him. No one ever demanded I do so" (38).

59. Phillip Brian Harper, *Abstractionist Aesthetics: Artistic Form and Social Critique in African American Culture* (New York: New York University Press, 2015), 127.

60. Coleman, 199.

Coda

1. Within a 5-mile radius of The World Stage, the population is 33.1% Latinx, and 32.8% Black. See The Urban Land Institute: Leimert Park Village. *Ridley-ThomasLACounty.gov*. Web. April 15, 2016.

2. Interview with Dwight Trible, March 2, 2016.

3. See programs at theworldstage.org.

4. Interview with Dwight Trible.

5. Interview with Dwight Trible.

Bibliography

Adams, Jenoyne. *Resurrecting Mingus*. New York: Free Press, 2001. Print.
Agamben, Giorgio. *Homo Sacer: Sovereign Power and Bare Life*. Trans. Daniel Heller-Roazen. Palo Alto, CA: Stanford University Press, 1998. Print
Amen I, Ra Un Nefer, *Metu Neter Vol. 1: The Great Oracle of Tehuti and the Egyptian System of Spiritual Cultivation*. Brooklyn: Kamit Publications, 1990. Print.
Anzaldúa, Gloria. *Borderlands/La Frontera: The New Mestiza*. San Francisco: Aunt Lute Books, 2007. Print.
Asante, Molefi Kete. *The Afrocentric Idea: Revised Edition*. Philadelphia: Temple University Press, 1998. Print.
Asante, Molefi Kete. *The Egyptian Philosophers: Ancient African voices from Imhotep to Akhenaten*. Chicago: African American Images, 2000. Print.
Awkward, Michael. *Negotiating Difference: Race, Gender and the Politics of Positionality*. Chicago: University of Chicago Press, 1995. Print.
Baker, Houston A. *Blues Ideology, and Afro-American Literature: A Vernacular Theory*. Chicago: University of Chicago, 1987. Print.
Baldwin, James. *The Fire Next Time*. New York: Dell, 1963. Print.
———. *Notes of a Native Son*. Boston: Beacon, 2012. Print.
Bambara, Toni Cade. *Deep Sightings and Rescue Missions*. New York: Vintage, 1999. Print.
———, ed. *The Black Woman: An Anthology*. New York: Signet, 1970. Print.
———. *The Salt Eaters*. New York: Vintage Books, 1980. Print.
Baraka, Amiri, & Larry Neal, eds. *Black Fire: An Anthology of Afro-American Writing*. New York: Morrow, 1968. Print.
Baraka, Amiri. *The Leroi Jones/Amiri Baraka Reader*. New York: Thunder's Mouth, 1991. Print.
Baraka, Ras, & Kevin Powell. *In the Tradition: An Anthology of Young Black Writers*. New York: Writers and Readers, 1992. Print.
Bennett, Jane. *The Enchantment of Modern Life: Attachments, Crossings, and Ethics*. Princeton, NJ: Princeton University Press, 2001. Print.

———. *Vital Matter: A political ecology of things*. Durham, NC, and London: Duke University Press, 2010. Print.

Blackwell, Maylei. *¡Chicana Power!: Contested Histories of Feminism in the Chicano Movement*. Austin: University of Texas Press, 2011. Print.

Brennan, Timothy. "From development to globalization: Postcolonial studies and globalization." *Postcolonial Literary Studies*. Ed. Neil Lazarus. Cambridge: Cambridge University Press, 2004. Print.

Brown, Simone. *Dark Matters: On the Surveillance of Blackness*. Durham, NC: Duke University Press, 2015. Print.

Buchanan, Shonda, ed. *Voices From Leimert Park: A Poetry Anthology*. Los Angeles: Tsehai Publishers, 2006. Print.

Budge, E. A. Wallis. *The Egyptian Book of the Dead*. Mineola, NY: Dover Publications, 1967. Print.

Butler, Octavia. *Kindred*. Boston: Beacon, 2004. Print.

Chen, Mel Y. *Animacies: Biopolitics, Racial Mattering, and Queer Affect*. Durham, NC, and London: Duke University Press, 2012. Print.

Christian, Barbara. *Black Feminist Criticism: Perspectives on Black Women Writers*. New York: Teachers College Press, 1985. Print.

———. *New Black Feminist Criticism, 1985–2000*. Eds. Bowles, Gloria, M. Giulia Fabi, & Arlene R. Keizer. Urbana: University of Illinois Press, 2007.

———. "The Race for Theory." *Cultural Critique* 6 (1987): 51–63.

Cisneros, Sandra. *Woman Hollering Creek*. New York: Vintage, 1991. Print.

Coleman, Wanda. *Heavy Daughter Blues: Poems & Stories 1968–1986*. Santa Rosa, CA: Black Sparrow Press, 1987. Print.

———. *The Riot Inside Me: More Trials & Tremors*. Jaffrey, NH: Black Sparrow Books, 2005. Print.

Compact Edition of the Oxford English Dictionary, The. 1997. Print.

Cone, James H. *The Spirituals & the Blues*. New York: The Seabury Press, 1972. Print.

Crenshaw, Kimberlé. "Demarginalizing the Intersection of Race and Sex: A Black Feminist Critique of Antidiscrimination Doctrine, Feminist Theory and Ant-Racist Politics." *The University of Chicago Legal Forum* (1989): 139–68.

Crossan, John Dominic. *The Cross That Spoke: The Origins of the Passion Narrative*. New York: Harper Collins, 1992. Print.

Cruse, Harold. *The Crisis of the Negro Intellectual*. New York: William Morrow, 1967. Print.

Daáood, Kamau. *The Language of Saxophones: Selected Poems of Kamau Daáood* San Francisco: City Lights, 2005. Print.

Davis, Angela Y. *Women, Race & Class*. New York: Vintage, 1983. Print.

———. *Angela Davis: An Autobiography*. New York: International, 1989. Print.

———. *Freedom is Constant Struggle: Ferguson, Palestine and the Foundations of a Movement*. Chicago: Haymarket Books, 2016. Print.
Del Castillo, Richard Griswold. *The Treaty of Guadalupe Hidalgo*. Norman: University of Oklahoma Press, 1990. Print.
Derrida, Jacques. *Rogues: Two Essays on Reason*. Trans. Pascale-Anne Brault and Michael Naas. Palo Alto, CA: Stanford University Press, 2005. Print.
Du Bois, W. E. B. *The Souls of Black Folk*. New York: Dover, 1994. Print.
Douglass, Frederick. *Narrative of the Life of Frederick Douglass, An American Slave*. Hollywood, FL: Simon and Brown, 2013. Print.
Echols, Alice. *Daring to Be Bad: Radical Feminism in America 1967–1975*. Minneapolis: University of Minnesota Press, 1989. Print.
Edwards, Brent Hayes. *The Practice of Diaspora: Literature, Translation, and the Rise of Black Internationalism*. Cambridge, MA: Harvard University Press, 2003. Print.
Edwards, Erica R. *Charisma and the Fictions of Black Leadership*. Minneapolis: University of Minnesota Press, 2012. Print.
Elam, Jr., Harry J. *Taking It to the Streets: The Social Protest Theater of Luis Valdez and Amiri Baraka*. Ann Arbor: University of Michigan Press, 2001. Print.
Ellis, Trey. "The New Black Aesthetic." *Callaloo* 12, no. 1 (1989): 233–43.
Ellison, Ralph. *Invisible Man*. New York: Vintage, 1952. Print.
Erman, Adolph. *Life in Ancient Egypt*. Mineola, NY: Dover Publications, 1971. Print.
Fanon, Frantz. *The Wretched of the Earth*. New York: Black Cat, 1968. Print.
———. *Black Skin, White Masks: Revised Edition*. New York: Grove Press, 2008.
Forché, Carolyn. "Twentieth Century Poetry of Witness." *American Poetry Review* 22:2 (March–April 1993): 9–16.
Foucault, Michel. *The History of Sexuality, Volume 1: An introduction*. New York: Knopf, 1990. Print.
———. *Michel Foucault: Aesthetics, Method and Epistemology*. Ed. James Faubion. New York: The New Press, 1998. 175–85. Print.
———. *"Society Must Be Defended": Lectures at the Collége de France, 1975–76*. Eds. Mauro Bertani & Alessandro Fontana. New York: Picador, 2003. Print.
Fraser, Nancy. "Rethinking the Public Sphere: A Contribution of the Critique of Actually Existing Democracy." *Social Text* 25/26 (1990): 56–80.
Freire, Paulo. *Pedagogy of the Oppressed*. New York: Continuum, 1996. Print.
Fuller, Charles. *A Soldier's Play*. New York: Hill and Wang, 1982. Print.
Fuss, Diana. *Essentially Speaking: Feminism, Nature, and Difference*. New York: Routledge, 1989. Print.
Gates, Jr., Henry Louis. *The Signifying Monkey: A Theory of Afro-American Literary Criticism*. New York: Oxford Press USA, 1989. Print.

Gayle, Jr., Addison, ed. *The Black Aesthetic*. New York: Doubleday, 1971. Print.
Gilbert, Derrick. *From Watts to Leimert Park: Two Generations of African American Poetry Movements in Los Angeles*. Dissertation, University of California. Los Angeles. 1998. Print.
Gilroy, Paul. *The Black Atlantic: Modernity and Double-Consciousness*. Cambridge, MA: Harvard University Press, 1993. Print.
Goodman, Steve. *Sonic Warfare: Sound, Affect, and the Ecology of Fear*. London: MIT Press, 2010. Print.
Greenlee, Sam. *The Spook Who Sat by the Door*. Detroit, MI: Wayne State University Press, 1989. Print.
Guevara, Ernesto. *Socialism and Man in Cuba*. Atlanta, GA: Pathfinder Press, 2009. Print.
Gutiérrez, Gustavo. *A Theology of Liberation: History Politics and Salvation*. Trans. Caridad Inda. Ossining, NY: Orbis Books, 1988. Print.
Habermas, Jürgen. *The Structural Transformation of the Public Sphere: An Inquiry into a Category of Bourgeois Society*. Trans. Thomas Burger. Cambridge, MA: MIT Press, 1991. Print.
Hall, Stuart. *Cultural Representations and Signifying Practices*. London: Sage Publications, 1997. Print.
Hansberry, Lorraine. *A Raisin in the Sun*. New York: Vintage, 2004. Print.
Harper, Phillip Brian. *Abstractionist Aesthetics: Artistic Form and Social Critique in African American Culture*. New York: New York University Press, 2015. Print.
Harris, Duchess. "From the Kennedy Commission to the Combahee Collective: Black Feminist Organizing, 1960–1980," *Sisters in the Struggle: African American Women in the Civil Rights-Black Power Movement*. Eds. Bettye Collier-Thomas & V. P. Franklin. New York: NYU Press, 2001. 282–88.
Harvey, David. *A Brief History of Neoliberalism*. Oxford: Oxford University Press, 2005. Print.
Hegel, G. W. F. *The Philosophy of Art*. Trans. William Hastie. New York: Barnes & Noble, 2006. Print.
Herbin, Fracois R. *Books of Breathing and Related Texts, Vol. 4*. London: British Museum Press, 2008. Print.
Himes, Chester. *If He Hollers Let Him Go*. New York: Da Capo, 2002. Print.
Hine, Darlene Clark, & John McCluskey, Jr. *The Black Chicago Renaissance*. Champaign: University of Illinois, 2012. Print.
Holland, Sharon Patricia. *Raising the Dead: Readings of Death and (Black) Subjectivity*. Durham, NC: Duke University, 2000. Print.
Hooks, Bell. *Ain't I A Woman: Black Women & Feminism*. Boston: South End, 1999. Print.
Hughes, Langston. *The Weary Blues*. New York: Knopf, 1945. Print.
Hull, Gloria T., Patricia Bell Scott, & Barbara Smith, eds. *All the Women Are White, All the Blacks Are Men, But Some of Us Are Brave: Black*

Women's Studies. New York: The Feminist Press at City University of New York, 1982. Print.
Hurston, Zora Neale. *Their Eyes Were Watching God*. New York: Harper Perennial, 2006. Print.
Jackson, Lawrence P. *The Indignant Generation: A Narrative History of African American Writers and Critics, 1934–1960*. Princeton, NJ: Princeton University Press, 2011. Print.
Jahn, Janheinz. *Muntu: African Culture and the Western World*. New York: Grove Press, 1990. Print.
Jarrett, Gene Andrew. *Representing the Race: A New Political History of African American Literature*. New York: New York University Press, 2011. Print.
Johnson, Gay Theresa. *Spaces of Conflict, Sounds of Solidarity: Music, Race and Spatial Entitlement in Los Angeles*. Berkeley: University of California Press, 2013. Print.
Johnson, Walter. *River of Dark Dreams: Slavery and Empire in the Cotton Kingdom*. Cambridge, MA: Harvard University Press, 2013. Print.
Jordan, June, *Passion: New Poems, 1977–1980*. Boston: Beacon, 1980. Print.
———. *Some of Us Did Not Die: New and Selected Essays of June Jordan*. New York: Basic Civitas, 2003. Print.
Kelly, Robin D. G. *Race Rebels: Culture, Politics, and the Black Working Class*. New York: Free Press, 1994. Print.
———. *Freedom Dreams: The Black Radical Imagination*. Boston: Beacon Press, 2002. Print.
Kohn, Margaret. *Radical Space: Building the House of the People*. Ithaca, NY: Cornell University Press, 2003. Print.
Larsen, Nella. *Passing*. New York: Random House, 2002. Print.
Latour, Bruno. *Pandora's Hope: Essays on the Reality of Science Studies*. Cambridge, MA: Harvard University Press, 1999. Print.
Leach, Neal, ed. *Rethinking Architecture: A Reader in Cultural Theory*. New York: Routledge, 1997. Print.
Levine, Lawrence. *Black Culture and Black Consciousness: Afro-American Folk Thought from Slavery to Freedom*. New York: Oxford Press USA, 1977. Print.
Lipsitz, George. *How Racism Takes Place*. Philadelphia: Temple University Press, 2011. Print
Locke, Alain, ed. *The New Negro*. New York: Touchstone, 1999. Print.
López, Tiffany A. *Growing Up Chicana/o*. New York: Harper Collins, 2009. Print.
Lorde, Audre. *Our Dead Behind Us*. New York: Norton, 1994. Print.
———. *Sister Outsider: Essays and Speeches*. New York: Crossing Press, 2007. Print.
Lowe, Lisa. *Immigrant Acts: On Asian American Cultural Politics*. Durham NC: Duke University Press, 1996. Print.

Mantler, Gordon K. *Power to the Poor: Black-Brown Coalition & the Fight for Economic Justice, 1960–1974*. Chapel Hill: University of North Carolina Press, 2013. Print.

Marren, Susan. "Between Slavery and Freedom: The Transgressive Self in Olaudah Equiano's Autobiography." *PMLA* 108.1 (1993): 94–105.

Marx, Karl. *The Marx-Engels Reader*. 2nd Edition. Ed. Robert C. Tucker. New York: Norton & Company, 1978. Print.

McKittrick, Katherine. *Demonic Grounds: Black Women and the Cartographies of Struggle*. Minneapolis: University of Minnesota, 2006. Print.

———. "Mathematics Black Life." *The Black Scholar: Journal of Black Studies and Research* 44. no. 2 (2014): 16–28.

McRuer, Robert. "A Visitation of Difference: Randall Kenan and Black Queer Theory." *Journal of Homosexuality* 26, nos. 2 and 3 (1993): 221–32.

Melamed, Jodi. *Represent and Destroy: Rationalizing Violence in the New Racial Capitalism*. Minneapolis: University of Minnesota Press, 2011. Print.

Moraga, Cherríe. *Heroes and Saints & Other Plays*. Albuquerque, NM: West End Press, 1994. Print.

———. *Loving in the War Years*. Boston: South End Press, 2000. Print.

Moraga, Cherríe, & Gloria Anzaldúa, eds. *This Bridge Called My Back: Writings by Radical Women of Color*. Berkeley, CA: Third Woman Press, 2002. Print.

Morrison, Toni. *Playing in the Dark: Whiteness and the Literary Imagination*. New York: Vintage, 1993. Print.

———. *Beloved*. New York: Vintage, 2004. Print.

———. *The Song of Solomon*. New York, 2004. Print.

———. *The Bluest Eye*. New York: Vintage, 2007. Print.

Moten, Fred. *In the Break: The Aesthetics of the Black Radical Tradition*. Minneapolis: University of Minnesota Press, 2012. Print.

Muller, Lauren and the Blueprint Collective, eds. *June Jordan's Poetry for the People: A Revolutionary Blueprint*. New York: Routledge, 1995. Print.

Mumford, Kevin J. "Homo Sex Changes: Race, Cultural Geography, and the Emergence of the Gay," *American Quarterly* 48. no. 3 (1996): 395–414.

Naylor, Gloria. *The Women of Brewster Place*. New York: Penguin. 1983. Print.

———. *Linden Hills*. New York: Penguin, 1987. Print.

Nunley, Vorris L. *Keepin' It Hushed: The Barbershop and African American Hush Harbor Rhetoric*. Detroit, MI: Wayne State University Press, 2011. Print.

Ong, Aihwa. *Neoliberalism as Exception: Mutations in Citizenship and Sovereignty*. Durham, NC: Duke University Press, 2006. Print.

Patterson, Orlando. *Slavery and Social Death: A Comparative Study*. Cambridge, MA: Harvard University Press, 1982. Print.

Pena, Elaine A. *Performing Piety: Making Space Sacred with the Virgin of Guadalupe*. Berkeley: University of California, 2011. Print.

Perkins-Valdez, Dolen. *Wench*. New York: Amistad, 2010. Print.
Pharr, Suzanne. *Homophobia: A Weapon of Sexism*. Berkeley, CA: Chardon Press, 1997. Print.
Pulido, Laura. *Black, Brown, Yellow and Left: Radical Activism in Los Angeles*. Berkeley: University of California Press, 2016. Print.
Plascencia, Salvador. *The People of Paper*. New York: Harvest Books, 2006. Print.
Quashe, Kevin. *The Sovereignty of Quiet: Beyond Resistance in Black Culture*. New Brunswick, NJ: Rutgers University Press, 2012. Print.
Redding, Arthur F. *Haints: American Ghosts, Millennial Passions, and Contemporary Gothic Fictions*. Tuscaloosa: University of Alabama Press, 2011. Print.
Redmond, Eugene. *Drumvoices: The Mission of Afro American Poetry: A Critical History*. New York: Anchor, 1976. Print.
Reed, Ishmael. *Mumbo Jumbo*. New York: Scribner, 1996. Print.
Reid-Pharr, Robert. *Once You Go Black: Choice, Desire, and the Black American Intellectual*. New York: New York University Press, 2007. Print.
Robinson, Cedric. *Black Movements in America*. New York: Routledge, 1997. Print.
———. *Black Marxism: The Making of the Black Radical Tradition*. Chapel Hill: University of North Carolina Press, 2000. Print.
Schulberg, Budd. *From the Ashes: Voices from Watts*. New York: New American Library, 1967. Print.
Segrest, Mab. *Memoir of a Race Traitor*. Boston: South End Press, 1993. Print.
Shakur, Assata. *An Autobiography*. New York: Lawrence Hill, 1987. Print.
Smith, Barbara. *The Truth That Never Hurts: Writings on Race, Gender and freedom*. New Brunswick, NJ: Rutgers University Press, 1998. Print.
Spillers, Hortense J. "Mama's Baby, Papa's Maybe: An American Grammar Book." *Diacritics* (Summer 1987): 65–81.
Squires, Catherine R. "Rethinking the Black Public Sphere: An Alternative Vocabulary for Multiple Public Spheres." *Communication Theory* 12:4 (2002): 446–68.
Steele, Shelby. *The Content of Our Character: A New Vision of Race in America*. New York: Harper Perennial, 1998. Print.
Tibebu, Teshale. *Hegel and the Third World: The Making of Eurocentrism in World History*. Syracuse, NY: Syracuse University Press, 2011. Print.
Troupe, Quincy. *Snake Back Solos: Selected Poems*. New York: I Reed Books, 1979. Print.
Von Baeyer, Hans Christian. *Warmth Disperses and Time Passes: The History of Heat*. New York: The Modern Library, 1999. Print.
Walker, Alice. *In Search of Our Mothers' Gardens: Womanist Prose*. New York: Mariner, 1983. Print.
———. *The Color Purple*. New York: Mariner, 2003. Print.
Walls, David. *Community Organizing*. Cambridge: Polity Press, 2015. Print.

Weheliye, Alexander G. *Habeous Viscous: Racializing Assemblages, Biopolitics and Black Feminist Theories of the Human*. Durham, NC: Duke University Press, 2014. Print.

Woods, Clyde. *Development Arrested: The Blues and Plantation Power in the Mississippi Delta*. Brooklyn: Verso Books, 2017. Print

Wynter, Sylvia. "Human Being as Noun? Being Human as Praxis? Towards the Autopoetic Turn/Overturn: A Manifesto." Accessed 4 March, 2018. https://www.scribd.com/document/329082323/Human-Being-as-Noun-Or-Being-Human-as-Praxis-Towards-the-Autopoetic-Turn-Overturn-A-Manifesto#from_embed

———. "Towards the Sociogenic Principle: Fanon, The Puzzle of Conscious Experience, of 'Identity' and What it's Like to be 'Black.'" Accessed 6 March, 2018. http://coribe.org/PDF/wynter_socio.pdf

West, Cornel. *The Cornel West Reader*. New York: Basic Civitas, 2000. Print.

Widener, Daniel. *Black Arts West: Culture and Struggle in Post-War Los Angeles*. Durham, NC: Duke University Press, 2010. Print.

Wilson, August. *Fences*. New York: Plume, 1996. Print.

Wright, Richard. *Native Son*. New York: Perennial Classics, 2005. Print.

Yarbo-Bejarano, Yvonne. *The Wounded Heart: Writing on Cherríe Moraga*. Austin: University of Texas Press, 2001. Print.

Ziarek, Ewa Plonowska. *Impasses of the Post-Global: Theory in the Era of Climate Change*. Vol. 2. Ed. Henry Sussman. London: Open Humanities Press, 2012. 194–211. Print.

Index

actant, 10, 11, 12, 14, 15, 43, 50, 52, 54, 56, 96, 150
activist, 6, 7, 12, 13, 14, 20, 21, 31, 33, 34, 35, 36, 42, 48, 49, 61, 63, 65, 71, 72, 75, 76, 79, 80, 87, 88, 89, 91, 94, 97, 115, 131, 136, 137
Agamben, Giorgio, 4, 5, 51, 140
Alatorre, Chloe, 25
animacy, 7–12, 15, 34, 35, 39, 40, 43, 52, 54, 58, 59, 63, 65, 83, 84, 87, 91, 92, 93, 106, 107, 109, 111, 112, 115, 118, 119, 126
ankh, 15, 20, 21, 22, 23, 39, 40, 41
ankhing, 14, 15, 19, 20, 23, 24, 26, 30, 32, 33, 34, 35, 37, 39, 40, 44, 45, 48, 50, 63, 75, 79, 93, 95, 96, 97, 98, 100, 101, 115, 136
Anzaldúa, Gloria, 1, 5, 6, 10, 37, 94, 97
"Army of Healers" (Daáood), 118, 119, 120, 121, 123, 125, 126, 127
artistic heterotopias of resistance, 31, 33, 59, 60, 96, 101, 105, 106
Asante, Molefi Kete, 15

Baldwin, James, 118, 119
Bambara, Toni Cade, 6, 14, 15, 21, 23, 31, 33, 36, 63, 93

"bare life," 3–7, 9, 11, 15, 34, 37, 39, 40, 41, 42, 43, 46, 47, 50, 51, 52, 53, 59, 63, 66, 69, 70, 71, 74, 77, 78, 82, 83, 84, 87, 89, 91, 92, 93, 103, 107, 109, 113, 115, 118, 119, 120, 121, 122, 123, 124, 125, 126, 128, 129, 130
Bennett, Jane, 7, 8, 9, 10, 11, 12, 54, 55, 89
Berkeley, University of California, 99, 101
biopolitics, 4, 108
Black Lives Matter, 11
Blackwell, Maylei, 25, 96
Bland, Sandra, 3, 139, 140
blues, 16, 17, 18, 19, 51, 55, 117, 118, 120, 121, 123, 125, 126, 127, 128, 133
Brennan, Timothy, 14
Brisbon, Rumain, 3
Brown, Michael, 2, 4, 5, 9

canon, 36, 93, 95, 97, 99, 101, 102, 103, 104, 105, 115
Castile, Philando, 5, 140
Centro de Acción Social Autónomo (CASA), 25
Chapman, Kindra, 3
Chen, Mel Y., 7, 8, 9, 10, 11, 13, 43, 106, 108, 109, 111

169

Chin, Marilyn, 103
Christian, Barbara, 99
Clark, Stephon, 5, 141
Coleman, Wanda, 6, 37, 118, 127, 128, 129, 130, 132, 133
Cone, James H., 16, 17, 18, 27, 30, 51, 55, 80, 118
Corona, Bert, 25
counterpublic, 6, 14, 15, 19, 20, 25, 26, 27, 28, 35, 59, 63, 64, 65, 66, 69, 76, 93, 96, 98, 99, 100, 101, 104, 105, 107, 115, 135
Crenshaw, Kimberlé, 130, 131
Curnell, Joyce, 3

Daáood, Kamau, 6, 37, 53, 56, 115, 117, 118, 119
Davis, Angela Y., 96, 97
Del Castillo, Richard Griswold, 112, 155
Derrida, Jaques, 69
Douglass, Frederick, 34

Edwards, Brent Hayes, 93, 94
Edwards, Erica R., 6, 13, 20, 35, 37, 137

Fanon, Frantz, 8, 16
Ferguson (Missouri), 2
Forché, Carolyn, 120, 133, 157
Ford, Ezell, 3
Forman, Ruth, 99
Foucault, Michel, 4, 28, 29, 65, 70, 75, 140, 144
Fraser, Nancy, 24, 25, 64, 65, 98
Freire, Paulo, 105, 106, 107, 108, 111, 113, 115

Garner, Eric, 3, 4, 5
Gates, Jr., Henry Louis, 53
Guevara, Ernesto "Che,"1
Gurley, Akai, 3

Habermas, Jürgen, 24
Hamilton, Dontre, 3
Harjo, Joy, 99
Harper, Phillip Brian, 132
Harris, Duchess, 44, 148
Harvey, David, 14
Hegel, G. W. F., 19
Heroes and Saints, 36, 65, 66, 69, 71, 73, 77, 80, 84, 86, 87, 88, 120
heterotopias (Foucault), 28
heterotopias of resistance (Kohn), 28, 29, 30, 31, 59, 65, 66, 69, 75, 76, 79, 80, 95, 96, 97, 98, 99, 100, 101, 104, 107, 147
hieroglyphics of the flesh (Spillers), 64, 65, 66, 69, 71, 87, 114, 122, 123, 124, 126–130, 133
homo sacer, 4, 5, 54
Holland, Sharon Patricia, 22
Hughes, Langston, 31
hush harbor, 17, 18, 35, 131, 144, 149

"Identifying Marks" (Coleman), 127, 129, 132, 133, 159
improvisation, 31, 40, 52, 53

jazz, 53, 55, 56, 135
Jones, Ralkina, 3
Jordan, June, 6, 37, 94, 98, 99, 101, 104, 105, 106, 107, 108, 111, 113
June Jordan's Poetry for the People, 37, 94, 98, 99, 101, 104, 105, 106, 107, 113, 152

Keunang, Charly Leundeu, 3
Kohn, Margaret, 28, 29, 30, 59, 65, 66, 75, 80, 95, 96, 97, 100

La facultad, 1

Lamar, Kendrick, 56
Latour, Bruno, 10, 52
Leimert Park, 135, 160
Lipsitz, George, 12, 99, 118, 142, 143
López, Tiffany, 32
Lorde, Audre, 19, 20, 30, 70, 80, 99
Lowe, Lisa, 110, 112, 113, 155

Martin, Trayvon, 2, 9
Marx, Karl, 9, 43, 110
McKittrick, Katherine, 5, 7
"mere life," 4, 6
Mexican American Political Association, 25
Moraga, Cherríe, 6, 23, 36, 37, 65, 94, 95, 97, 113, 114
Moten, Fred, 18, 40, 42, 52, 123
Muller, Lauren, 37, 101
Mumbo Jumbo, 36, 40, 51, 53, 57, 60
Mu'tafikah, 57, 58, 59
mutualista, 25

Nunley, Vorris, L., 35, 144

Ong, Aihwa, 14, 66

People of Paper, The, 14, 15, 36, 40, 41, 44, 51, 60, 67
Plascencia, Salvador, 6, 14, 15, 36, 38, 40
Pulido, Laura, 25

Redding, Arthur, 33
Reed, Ishmael, 6, 36, 39, 40, 51, 58, 59
Rich, Adrienne, 99, 101, 102, 103
Robinson, Cedric, 1

Salt Eaters, The, 6, 14, 15, 23, 31, 33, 34, 36, 63, 65, 92, 118
Shange, Ntozake, 99, 132
Smith, Barbara, 21, 94, 95, 153
sociogenic, 8
sovereign, 3–7, 37, 41, 42, 43, 45, 47, 49, 50, 63, 67, 69, 70, 71–79, 81–89, 91, 92, 93, 98, 100, 102, 103, 106, 107, 108, 109, 113, 120, 126, 131, 140
Spillers, Hortense J., 4, 11, 63, 64, 123, 124
Spirit, 14–19, 26–31, 33, 35, 37, 40, 51, 52, 53, 54, 55, 56, 57, 63, 80, 82, 89, 115
Squires, Catherine R., 25, 26, 27, 28, 64, 65, 69, 100

This Bridge Called My Back, 36, 94, 96, 97, 98, 113, 152
Treaty of Guadalupe Hidalgo, 112, 113, 155
Trible, Dwight, 56, 135
Trump, Donald J., 3, 111–113, 140
Turner, Nat, 11
Turner, Raynette, 3

Valerio, Max Wolf, 113, 114
Vibrations (venue), 2, 20, 25
Virgen de Guadalupe, 76, 77, 90, 152

Walker, Alice, 131, 132, 159
Weheliye, Alexander G., 4, 64, 69
Wells, Ida B., 11
Woods, Clyde, 17, 18, 120, 145
World Stage Performance Gallery, The, 56, 135, 136
Wynter, Slylvia, 8, 9

Ziarek, Ewa Plonowska, 4, 6, 11, 15

www.ingramcontent.com/pod-product-compliance
Lightning Source LLC
Chambersburg PA
CBHW030827230426
43667CB00008B/1419